THE
GREAT WESTERN RAILWAY'S
LAST LOOK FORWARD

A NEW MEDIUM SIZE STATION

THE WAITING ROOM

THE
GREAT WESTERN RAILWAY'S
LAST LOOK FORWARD

being a reprint of
NEXT STATION
by Christian Barman

DAVID & CHARLES
NEWTON ABBOT

ISBN 0 7153 5720 4

First published by the Great Western Railway in conjunction
with George Allen & Unwin Limited, 1947, under the title
NEXT STATION

This edition © British Railways Western Region 1972
© New introduction Christian Barman 1972

Note: The seven illustrations based on artists' impressions,
originally in colour,
have been reproduced in black and white in this reprint

Printed in Great Britain by
Latimer Trend & Co Ltd Whitstable Kent for
David & Charles (Publishers) Ltd.
Newton Abbot Devon

PREFATORY NOTE
TO THE 1972 EDITION

IN the summer of 1946 when this little book was started the railway managements were busy trying to do three things all at once, make good the ravages of another world war, work out a development programme, and consider how this programme was likely to be affected by the process of nationalisation. They had known about nationalisation since the Attlee Government came to power twelve months earlier, but it was not till the end of 1946 that the Government confirmed that the railways were down in the list and due to be dealt with in the course of that Session. If the prospect brought a sense of despondency to many Great Westerners, it was not so much because they disliked the idea of State enterprise as because the decision had been made by people who were not interested in the railways and their troubles; all they wanted was to nationalise a few things. The deplorable lack of ideas about the future made it seem more than ever necessary that the railways should themselves press forward with their planning and make these plans known to their staffs, customers and friends. The Great Western's Chairman, Viscount Portal of Laverstoke, had had a good deal to say upon the subject when he addressed the Annual Meeting held in March 1946 and later in that year I was asked to develop and expand his statement and produce a permanent record for publication.

Work had not been going on very long before it became clear that the book when it came out would look more like a valedictory gesture than a programme for future work. The thought tempted me to introduce another little valedictory note which may still be of interest to readers of the present edition. My friend Thomas Edgar Griffits (1883-1957), the last and greatest of the old school of craftsman lithographers employed in the printing trade, was due to retire from practical work before the end of 1947. It was arranged that the artists' drawings for the seven colour illustrations should be copied by him on lithographic plates. The original edition of *Next Station* must be one of the very last books to be printed in this country with illustrations hand-copied in the workshop by this traditional craft technique. Although in the present edition they are reproduced the modern way (and in black and white) the observant reader will easily recognise the old craftsman's sensitive strokes, printed in facsimile with no reduction in scale.

The Great Western Railway finally made its exit on the last day of December 1947 when the entire body of directors vanished overnight together with Sir James Milne, the leading figure in the British railway industry; though only a little over sixty years old he had been a director and the general manager of the Company for nearly twenty years. The only people who seemed happy about the vacuum thus left at the top of all four railways (now increased to five) were our legislators who had already made up their minds that the posts of general manager should be abolished so that the management function might be centralised at a national headquarters. It was not, of course, their fault that the only available candidate for the post of railway chief was a junior person with little experience of peace-time management. And so life went on till the summer of 1953 when the Churchill Government had been in office for a couple of years.

Churchill himself was known to have a special affection for the railways. He had seen how they had exerted themselves in two wars and what they had suffered; the politician in him as well as the private citizen believed that no time must be lost putting them on their feet again. At that moment General Sir Brian Robertson, later Lord Robertson of Oakridge, was in Cairo engaged in negotiations with the Egyptian Government. He was a soldier, business leader and statesman who a few years earlier had further added to his stature as administrator (and doubtless also to his understanding of the problems of railway modernisation) during his period as the British Member of the Allied High Commission in Germany. The letter from Downing Street started with a question: 'How would you like to command an army of a million men?' The arithmetic was perhaps a little sketchy but the message seemed clear enough. At the opening of the new Session of Parliament, Churchill was speaking in the debate on the Address; when he came to the subject of the railways and Sir Brian Robertson's appointment he explained how he and his colleagues, having regretfully come to the conclusion that the railways had better carry on as a nationalised concern, were yet determined to do 'our utmost' for them. A few weeks later Sir Brian took up his post and the spirit that had moved the Great Western to take this hopeful look forward started to come alive again.

CHRISTIAN BARMAN

CONTENTS

INTRODUCTION

THIS BOOK is a study of initiative in action as exemplified in a famous English railway. The subject is not without special interest in these times. "The well-being of a community," wrote a great modern student of the science of business administration, "finally depends on the degree to which initiative is exercised and organised." Those words, as far as this country is concerned, have become conspicuously an understatement. To exercise and organise initiative is for us to-day less a means of attaining well-being than a condition of our survival as a free people. If ever there was a time for initiative, this is that time.

The railways of England are not unfamiliar with the kind of situation where initiative means the difference between extinction and survival. Every schoolboy knows how their introduction was resisted by the embattled forces of reaction and greed. The famous remark of Lord de Mowbray in Disraeli's *Sybil*, "you may depend upon it that these railroads are very dangerous things", was echoed in every corner of the land. The force of initiative brought them safely through; the same force made possible a record of continuous development that placed them, upon the outbreak of the first German war, at the head of all the world's railways for safety, speed and regularity. It is hardly surprising that their position in this country should be unlike that of any other country's railway system. Elsewhere, railways arrived as gasworks and safety razors arrived; of England alone can it be said that railways are part of the history of the nation. Where is there another people that speaks of the Railway Age as the French speak of the Age of Louis XIV? The names of Brunel and Stephenson live beside those of Drake and Hawkins. As examples of creative initiative, our railways are unequalled in modern industrial history. Their significance is more than national. "Railways," says G. M. Trevelyan, "were England's gift to the world."

It is a distinguishing mark of initiative that it should set itself the highest possible standards. The standards of the Great Western Railway have been set high since the beginning. "I am thus engineer to the finest work in England," wrote Brunel in his diary. The date of this entry is significant: it was written on Boxing Day, 1835. Nothing was built; nothing had been started; all that had happened was that Parliament had passed the Great Western Railway Act. Brunel was doing the same thing that is attempted in these pages; he was looking forward into the future; "the finest work" was that which existed at that moment only in his own brain and heart. A few years later he put into one of his reports a fuller statement of his intentions. "It will," he wrote,

[1] T. N. Whitehead, in *Leadership in a Free Society* (1936).

I

"be the fault of the Company if it does not effectually and permanently secure to itself the whole trade of this portion of England, with that of South Wales and the south of Ireland; not by a forced monopoly, which could never long resist the wants of the public, but by such attention to those wants as shall render any competition unnecessary and hopeless." Other commercial entrepreneurs have shown themselves unafraid of competition; there have even been some who have welcomed it. But where is there another example of the possibility of effective competition being thus dismissed with an assurance amounting to contempt? Where your aims are the highest that are humanly attainable, those of the other fellow cease to signify.

It was, then, in such a mood that there took place the inception of the Railway that was to be the first in the world to build eight-wheeled passenger coaches (1881), to build modern full-length passenger coaches (1905), to connect all coaches by corridor (1892), to run a regular train service without a stop for over 240 miles (1904), to run a steam train at a speed exceeding 100 m.p.h. (1904); the first in Great Britain to introduce superheating of locomotive steam (1906), to build the powerful modern 4-6-2 ("Pacific") type of locomotive (1908), the first to apply modern scientific methods to locomotive design by studying train resistance in a specially built dynamometer car (1848) and by testing locomotives under controlled "laboratory" conditions (1904). This is not the place in which to enumerate the whole of the Railway's pioneering developments, which are familiar to all students of railway history. It may, however, be remarked that the most interesting thing about these achievements is the far-reaching chain of consequences that has flowed from so many of them. An astonishing number of the ideas that have come from the Great Western have been germinal ideas whose influence in the country at large has far exceeded that which they were able to exert in their own original environment. One or two current examples will illustrate this curious point.

The first example is the modern conception of road transport as an essential ancillary of transport by rail. As one of the pioneers of the motor bus, the Great Western was the first railway to run bus services as feeders to its stations. Its first bus service was started in Cornwall in August, 1903. This was the year before the first L.G.O.C. bus appeared on the streets of London, and nine years before the first London bus service was brought into correlation with the railway. At about the same time it inaugurated the Country Lorry Service which first introduced the systematic use of road-rail transport as an integral service for the rapid door-to-door carriage of goods over long distances. This conception was made the basis of the important discussions between the railways and the National Road Transport Federation which were initiated in May, 1945. The Federation, a representative body covering the interests of those road hauliers whose activities parallel those of the railways, stated that the road haulage industry was prepared to assume the obligations attaching to the functions of a public transport service in the full sense of the word. In July, 1946, an agreed scheme for the co-ordination of all road and rail freight transport was submitted to the Government. The Government has since rejected the scheme, but the case for a co-ordinated service has been overwhelmingly established, and by one means or another the principle is certain to be given practical application during the next few years.

For a second example we may take the development of oil firing for steam locomotives not as an emergency measure but as part of a normal operational programme. It was largely this bold innovation that made possible the Government's general campaign for the wider use of oil fuel which was first announced in July, 1946. In the middle of August, the Government stated that the railways had been instructed to convert some twelve hundred locomotives to oil firing, with a prospective saving, when the programme is complete, of one million tons of coal a year. It is not known at this moment whether the Government campaign is, or is not, a part of a comprehensive long-term plan; but there is no doubt whatever about the significance of the Railway's original programme of the previous year. Its purpose was not only to effect a saving of coal by the use of an alternative fuel, but to make each locomotive perform the maximum amount of useful work, to simplify and reduce the labour involved in locomotive servicing, and to eliminate the heavy physical toil of manual stoking.

Perhaps the most interesting thing about these two examples of causes and effects is their reference to the broader social activities with which a modern railway is inextricably linked. A railway like the Great Western is not a machine working in isolation from other machines. Above all, it is necessary always to remember that much of the work of a British railway undertaking is done in partnership with the other railways. This partnership is one of long standing. Where the quality of the service demands it, the railways have never hesitated to put aside private interest in organising work as a combined operation to a mutually agreed plan.

It was in the year 1842, when the Great Western was but seven years old, that British railways set the world an example in industrial co-ordination by creating the Railway Clearing House. One of the objects of this organisation, which has served the country well for over a century, was to enable passengers and customers for freight traffic to use the many companies' facilities in a single operation and at a single inclusive charge. The co-ordination of railway transport has developed in many directions since those early days. There is, for example, the well-established system for the interchange of freight wagons throughout the entire British network which was first introduced during the first world war. Under this system, administered by the Common User Committee of the freight rolling stock controllers, each railway drew upon the common pool for a number of wagons equal to the number built and maintained by itself. During the recent war the Government, as a wartime measure, had to cause a great many things to be pooled, from soft drinks to retail traders' road vehicles, in the interests of economy. In the case of railway wagons this was not necessary. The pool – a national pool amounting to some 600,000 wagons in all – was already there. All the Government had to do was to add to it the wagons owned by the mining industry and other industries outside the railway field. The comprehensive system managed by the Inter-Company Freight Rolling Stock Control included roundly 1,100,000 freight vehicles, with 408,000 wagon sheets and 219,000 wagon lashing ropes. It worked perfectly throughout the war, and incidentally enabled the railways of this country to carry the astronomical total of 1,700 million tons of freight.

Taking another example on a purely local scale, one might consider the arrangements for goods transport by road in the London area. The system, which has been in operation since 1937, was designed in the first place for the collection and delivery of goods and parcels. The area covered is roundly 150 square miles. From its twelve goods stations and depots (one, the Poplar depot, is still out of action as a result of bomb damage) the Great Western's 531 modern motor vehicles and 163 horses carry traffic destined not only for its own trains but for those of all the four main line railways. Elsewhere in London the other three partners to the scheme serve their allotted areas in a similar way. An important part of the traffic goes to the great London markets; in 1945, the Great Western's share of this market traffic was over 55,000 tons, consisting as to nearly half of perishable foodstuffs carried by passenger train. In Inner London, the combined system also offers a purely local service which collects and delivers direct from door to door. Another part of the scheme provides for the joint carriage of goods and parcels from one main line station to another; to the pooled fleet of 127 vehicles used for this service in 1946, the Great Western contributed twenty-nine.

These few examples will illustrate the gradual development of many Great Western activities as part of a combined transport organisation working to a broad national plan. Close co-operation between the railways has borne fruit in other fields besides transport; it was, for example, the railways that by joint action prevailed upon the Government to establish Greenwich Mean Time as the official standard time for all parts of the country.

Yet for all this great field of co-operation which is steadily extending, the Great Western is still very conscious of its own not inconsiderable identity. Its name, the oldest of all railway names extant to-day, was given to it in 1833. True, its present constitution and physical aspect go back less than a quarter of a century. Ninety years after it got its name, an Act of Parliament added to its 87,000 workers the 21,000 men employed by thirty-two smaller railways. None the less, it remained, and remains to-day, unmistakably the Great Western. The continuity goes deeper than the mere outward symbol of a name. Two great wars have helped still further to strengthen the bonds that unite its far-flung family.

In August, 1921, crippled by war service and by the enforced postponement of repairs and renewals, the Railway was handed back by the Government to its owners.

4

INTRODUCTION

The years that followed were full of difficulty. The visions of reconstruction had faded, and a mood of disillusionment hung darkly over the land. The Railway, however, took up its increased responsibilities in a spirit of confidence and resolution. By renewed toil it finally made good the injuries inflicted by the war. The old standards of service, among the highest in the world, were patiently inculcated among the many new workers added to the old Great Western family. After the 1932 depression there followed a time of expansion and prosperity. The Railway did not share in that prosperity. Hampered and restricted by many Government controls, it had to hold its own against competitors who, unrestricted and uncontrolled, enjoyed every kind of advantage. The way was hard; the reward was disappointing. Nevertheless, very soon its name again stood higher than ever in the public esteem. When the Railway was mobilised for another war, its organisation and its physical equipment proved capable of exertions whose relative intensity are without a parallel in railway history.

Many figures could be quoted to illustrate the magnitude of the effort that was then called for. Since statistical returns during the war were reduced to the barest necessities, none of them represents fully the true state of affairs. Here, for what it is worth, is a single example. From the records for the year 1944 it is clear that the total number of passenger journeys on all railways[1] in that year was 84,700,000 greater than it was in the last year before the war. This was an increase of 7·11 per cent. But the increase in the number of journeys originating on the Great Western was very much greater than 7·11 per cent. – 47·62 per cent. is the exact figure. The Great Western system is not the biggest of the railways; some indication of its size may be gathered from the fact that, under the financial arrangements provided in the existing scheme of Government control, its share of the total payments made to the railways is approximately 16 per cent. No significant additions were made to pre-war equipment to take up this additional burden; on the contrary, the equipment generally was diminished and weakened from many different causes during the progress of the war.

The second German war has come and gone. Much of the ground that was recovered between the two wars has been lost again, and, as with the country generally, a good deal more has been lost besides. The men and women of the Great Western, both the old staff and their wartime helpers, have done a job with which they may well feel some satisfaction. Their record is second to none in the country. But this longer, fiercer war has left deeper scars than the last, for the Railway paid its due share of the high price of Allied victory. This time there are more injuries to be repaired, heavier sacrifices to be made good; moreover, the difficulties of rebuilding are infinitely greater. This indeed is an occasion calling for initiative to be exercised and organised. The account which follows will show what kind of a beginning has been made.

---

[1]"Originating" journeys': i.e., all journeys including those involving travel on more than one company's lines are counted once only.

CHAPTER ONE · THE PASSENGER SERVICE

THE RAILWAY GOES ON

THE GREAT WESTERN is fortunate among all railways both in the loveliness of the country it serves and in the manner of its approach to that country. To journey from London to Swindon is like driving through eighty miles of well-tended park; on the more distant stretches of line there are many miles of moorland and river scenery and, of course, the sea. As the magic of the West country place-names floats down from the loudspeakers over the vaulted aisles of Paddington, the traveller thrills with pleasurable anticipation. His exit from London does not disappoint him; it is agreeable and direct; a straight and level run up the green river valley. A railway lives by taking people from one place to other places. Were there ever such pleasant places as those of the Great Western? Truly, to any railway that cares for the well being of passengers a road of this quality is a priceless possession indeed.

None the less it has been truly said that in modern railways the greatest asset of all is a service that is accepted by the public as providing the full degree of speed, safety and comfort expected by the discerning traveller. Assets of this kind do not come as a gift from heaven; they have to be built up through many years of grinding toil in workshops and laboratories no less than on the track and in the yards. The men who created the Great Western did not begrudge this toil, and their achievements are part of railway history. Its services have set standards of fast and punctual running for all the world's railways. At the outbreak of war its reputation stood higher than ever before. To restore that high standard has been the Railway's first and greatest objective during the difficult and uncertain months since the long war ended.

It is no exaggeration to say that the quality in men and material on which the Railway's reputation rests was built up over many years of exertion. The needs of war required that this accumulated wealth should be ruthlessly expended. Six years of persistent overwork have taken their toll. Repairs and maintenance have been deferred beyond their due time; replacements and renovations have been suspended. The physical deterioration can and will be measured in terms of money cost. The loss in human energy and skill cannot be so measured; and no one can doubt that it will require even greater efforts to make good.

THE PASSENGER SERVICE

When a liner needs overhaul, she comes out of service and is laid up. When new machinery is being put into a factory, the factory closes. But the Great Western system cannot close even for a few hours. At the end of 1946, the Railway was between eighteen months and two years behind in its work on the rehabilitation and renewal of loco-motives and carriages, new and existing, and in its work on track, stations and other physical assets. Nevertheless, the Railway must go on.

But, it will be said, if the Great Western cannot close, surely there has been an easing of wartime stress and strain which should enable the work of rehabilitation to be pressed forward. Alas, there is no such relaxation; there is only more work. Govern-ment traffic arising directly out of the war remained heavy throughout 1946. It included many goods trains as well as leave trains and demobilisation trains for troops. Twelve months after the end of the war, Government trains still averaged over 250 a week. And they are very difficult trains to handle. Altogether, loaded passenger trains on the Great Western system travelled 1,700,000 more miles in 1945 than in 1944, and 1944 was more than hard enough. During the summer of 1946, many trains carried 70 per cent. more people than they did before the war; the increase is largely in long-distance travel and affects some sections of the line with excessive severity. Recently, in a typical week, a count was made of passengers travelling in long-distance trains from Paddington. The increase over the corresponding week in 1938 was 85 per cent. This increase was not caused by Government traffic alone. Civilians are travelling more than they used to. For the Christmas seasons of 1945 and 1946, the Railway ran more special trains for civilians than for the previous busiest Christmas in its history.

The travelling public does not always remember that while endeavouring to meet the needs of civilian travellers, the railways have been kept hard at work helping to wind up the war. And though winding up the war may be a hard and costly business, as the British taxpayer has been learning to his great cost, nevertheless the Railway must go on.

PUNCTUALITY

It is good to be able to announce improved train services; it is better to carry out to perfection that which has already been announced. For that reason, the Great Western is giving the restoration of its pre-war standard of time-keeping priority over all other improvements. Day after day, the causes of delay are studied and reported on by experts. Difficult trains, trains with a bad timekeeping record, are made the subject of detailed observation and research. The effect of such trains on services generally are followed through from station to station. Methods of reducing delay are developed to meet each individual case.

The work is not made easier by the fact that the principal causes of unpunctuality are beyond the immediate control of the Railway. The abnormal conditions of present-day railway operation are a major source of trouble; in some cases shortages of labour or material are to blame. In nearly every case the trouble can be traced back to a direct legacy of the years of war.

The greatest cause of delay is the condition of the locomotives. Abnormal wear and tear, and the necessity of keeping locomotives constantly at work with the minimum of repair, have resulted in considerable deterioration. The number of engine failures in traffic, although much less than in 1945, is still abnormally high. Whereas in the year 1938 Great Western passenger trains suffered a locomotive failure every 126,000 miles, in 1946 there was a failure every 40,000 miles – that is to say more than three times as often.

More directly injurious to punctual running is the shortage of good quality coal. Great Western locomotives were designed to use certain selected types and grades of fuel–usually those most readily available in the vicinity in which they normally work. To-day the Railway cannot select the coal most suitable for its purpose, and it has to make the best use of the supplies it can get. Unsuitable coal adds to the troubles of the fireman; there are few cases of bad timekeeping of trains in which the failure of the engine to steam properly is not one of the contributory causes.

Last but not least comes shortage of materials. These include a number of materials necessary for repair work. An example are the cast-iron chairs that secure the rails to the sleepers. In a normal year before the war, Great Western relaying gangs would use roundly 19,000 new cast-iron rail chairs. To make up wartime arrears of replacements, 25,000 chairs are needed annually for the next three years. Supplies since the end of the war have hardly exceeded half that amount: one-third fewer chairs have been received than were used in 1938 for normal replacement.

These distressing details are given at some length because the rate of progress cannot be assessed at its true value without some understanding of the difficulties. For progress, indeed, there has been. The Great Western is not in the habit of boasting of its achievements, still less of making optimistic forecasts about things to come. But early in 1946 the special efforts which had been made to improve timekeeping began to show interesting results. During a typical week in February, the average delay for all express services in and out of Paddington was little more than half the average for the same week in 1945 – 53.2 per cent., to be precise. In present-day circumstances, an improvement of this order represents a very considerable effort. Its only effect on the operating departments was to spur them to greater exertions still.

MORE AND FASTER TRAINS

Next in importance after timekeeping comes the reinstatement of the full pre-war train service, that is to say of the number and speed of trains as exemplified in the time-tables for 1939.

The number of trains that can be run is determined by the number of locomotives and coaches that are available for the job. Reference is made elsewhere to the shortage in both these essentials, and the subject need not be elaborated here. The number of trains is also dependent on speed and on quick starting. The more quickly a train can be got away from a station, the sooner will the track be clear for the following train. And speed, as we have seen, is limited by a variety of factors, of which not the least is the condition of the track.

With the Great Western, as with the other British railways, the safety of the traveller comes before everything else. Standards of design and maintenance are fixed to allow substantial margins, and their absolute observance is insisted on. During the war, it became necessary for the full stringency of track maintenance and renewal standards to be relaxed. Since all available resources of labour and material had to be transferred to the war effort, fewer rails and sleepers were replaced each year. The Railway had to do one of two things: it must either reduce the margin of safety or it must reduce the speed of trains. It reduced the speed of trains. The overriding need for conserving fuel also entered into this decision, but the fact remains that not until the arrears of renewal have been made up to the satisfaction of the Chief Engineer will it be possible for trains to run at pre-war speeds again. Meanwhile, the programme for the gradual increase in both the number and the speed of trains is being steadily and effectively pursued.

The records show that the rebuilding of peacetime services on the Great Western started on 7 May, 1945, with the fast Bristol train leaving Paddington at 5.5 p.m., and the morning express which left Cardiff at 8.0 a.m. reaching Paddington at 11.0 a.m. (only 15 minutes later than in 1939). On and after 10 June, 1945, a considerable number of additional local services were run, mainly to improve facilities for workers to visit the country and seaside. The Fishguard-Waterford route to Ireland was re-opened on 16 July, 1945 ; the Fishguard-Cork route on 13 August of the same year; each service had three trains weekly on alternate days. (The restoration of the Fishguard-Rosslare service had to be deferred till 1947.) The next development was the introduction on 1 October, 1945, of ten additional long-distance trains linking Paddington with Cheltenham and Swansea, the Midlands with Cardiff and Penzance, and Cardiff with Brighton. A further stage was reached with the provision in 1946 of many new local trains in the Middlesex area, including a late night stopping train from Paddington to Reading. On 4 March, 1946, new trains between Paddington and Wolverhampton, leaving Paddington at 9.0 a.m. and Wolverhampton at 4.25 p.m., did much to improve this important service for business men.

On Monday, 6 May, 1946 – two months earlier than in pre-war years – the Great Western summer service came into operation. At one stroke, the number of trains in the timetable was increased by 948; the daily train mileage went up by 21,000 miles above the figure for the previous May. The familiar Great Western slip coaches were brought into service again, and these, in combination with readjusted running schedules, made it possible for savings of anything up to eighty minutes to be made in the journey times of ninety services. For the first time for six years, two famous named trains reappeared in the timetable. The Cornish Riviera Express resumed its run (the longest run on the system without an advertised stop – 225½ miles between Paddington and Plymouth). The journey time to Plymouth was cut by 15 minutes and the time to Penzance by 25 minutes. The Torbay Express leaving Paddington and Torquay simultaneously at 12 noon again brought Torquay within four hours' journey time of London. The running of Sunday trains was resumed on seven branch lines where the war had made such trains impracticable.

How, then, did the train service stand at the end of the first year of European peace? The passenger service was still 20 per cent. below the pre-war level. Trains were faster, but pre-war speeds had not yet been fully restored; the Cornish Riviera Express, for example, still took thirty minutes longer to reach Penzance than it did in 1939. Accelerated running, shorter station stops and improved connections made travel quicker and more convenient. On certain sections of the system – and on none more than on the main line between Paddington and South Wales – services were approaching the pre-war standard of frequency. The total mileage run by loaded passenger trains was further increased for the height of the summer season – the figure for the week ended 17 August, 1946, was one-fifth higher than for the corresponding week in 1945. Regarded as a whole, the Great Western's effort was more than remarkable: it was unique. During that same week in August, the loaded passenger train mileage for all British railways was 27 per cent. below the pre-war level. Great Western mileage was only 17 per cent. below. And journeys were easier and pleasanter in every way. The summer services brought restaurant cars on an additional 25 weekday trains and buffet cars on four, so that the total number of weekday trains providing meals *en route* stood at 53 altogether.

THE HOLIDAY PUZZLE

As far as the ordinary level of traffic is concerned, it will be noted that the excessive overcrowding brought about by the war is fast disappearing; consistently faster indeed than some of the other hardships that have come to us since 1939. But there are still such things as traffic peaks to be provided against, and the Great Western is aware that the peaks in future will be more accentuated than ever before. One of these peaks in particular is causing the Railway the deepest concern: the summer holiday peak which rises to a nightmare intensity at the August Bank Holiday weekend.

Various estimates have been published of the probable volume of the future summer holiday movement in this country. In 1946, the number of workers enjoying holidays with pay was roundly fifteen million – nearly four times the pre-war figure.

AUGUST HOLIDAYS

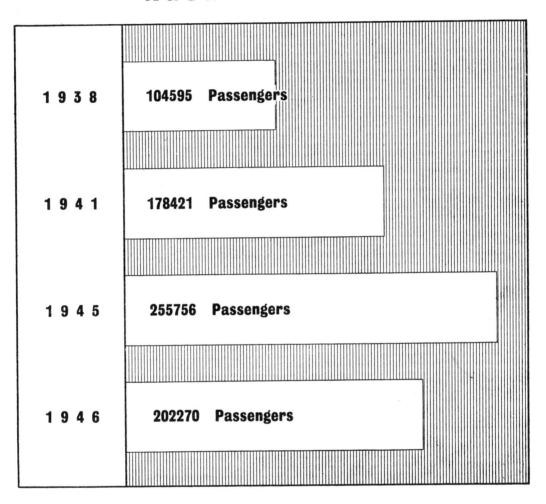

1938   104595 Passengers

1941   178421 Passengers

1945   255756 Passengers

1946   202270 Passengers

THE chart gives the number of passengers leaving Paddington station by long-distance trains during the third week in August – the weeks ending 20 August, 1938 (estimated), 23 August, 1941 (estimated), 25 August, 1945, and 24 August, 1946 respectively. The drop in the 1946 figure as compared with 1945 is largely due to the involuntary "staggering" of the holidays taken by men and women from the Services immediately after demobilisation.

The National Council of Social Service has made the conservative calculation that the eleven million new workers with their dependents will mean only eleven million new holiday makers; this figure is arrived at on the assumption that only half the new workers will leave home for a holiday and that there will be on an average one dependent accompanying every worker. Even on this modest basis, the number travelling will be virtually doubled. How are these numbers to be accommodated?

Holidays-with-pay is an admirable institution, but it needs other things besides pay to make it a practical reality. Unless some kind of staggering can be introduced, it is unlikely that the scheme can ever be put into full execution. An expert estimate published by P.E.P. in 1942[1] states that if there were no more staggering than before the war, the number of people seeking holiday accommodation at one time might rise to about five million. To provide comfortable transport for crowds of such a size would mean the building of thousands of locomotives and tens of thousands of coaches which would stand idle for ten months in the year. Can an efficiently managed railway provide facilities in such circumstances as these? A recent study sponsored by Nuffield College[2] states bluntly that "this is above the limit physically possible." Without some kind of staggering "many who could go away will be prevented, and essential services such as transport will be in danger of a complete breakdown."

Some indication of the trend of August holiday traffic is given in the chart on p. 11 which compares the number of passengers leaving Paddington during a typical August week (the third in the month) in 1938, 1941, 1945 and 1946. It will be seen that the position is growing progressively worse. The remedy lies in bold and comprehensive action by the Ministry of Education, by large municipalities and by the more important industrial organisations, so that as many holidays as possible may be spread over a season of five months. If the problem can be tackled with sufficient enterprise and drive, it should be possible, according to P.E.P., to reduce the peak figure of five million by something like half; but even this would be double the estimated pre-war peak of one and a quarter million. The means for securing comfortable holiday travel are really in the hands of the holidaymakers themselves. The people of this country mean to have more holidays and better holiday conditions, and they will get them provided all those on whom the timing of holidays depends can be persuaded to give their full share of co-operation.

SPECIAL FACILITIES

The Great Western passenger service before the war offered a number of special facilities designed to make travel by rail more comfortable and more economical. Among the most popular of these facilities was the reserved seat. For some years before

[1] *Planning for Holidays* : A Broadsheet issued by Political and Economic Planning
[2] Elizabeth Brunner : *Holiday Making and the Holiday Trades*. Oxford University Press, 1945

RESTAURANT CAR

1946

the war, this facility had shown a remarkable increase in popularity. Total annual reservations rose from just over a quarter of a million in 1929 to 423,600 in 1938; of this last total, 282,000 were for expresses from Paddington. The system involves the use of special staff and telephone lines; some idea of the pressure of work may be gained from the fact that on the Saturday of August Bank Holiday in 1939, 20,000 seats were reserved on trains from Paddington alone. Travellers have shown unmistakably the great value they put upon this service, and when the Government sanctioned its restoration on 7 October, 1946, it was a matter of regret to management and staff alike that it was possible for the time being to introduce it only on a dozen important trains.

Another facility the loss of which is widely felt is the whole range of reduced fare arrangements which brought greater freedom of movement to so many thousands of people before the war. Parents with young children in particular relied on them for easy access to the open air, to shopping centres and to places of amusement. Under the policy laid down by the Government, these facilities are being restored by slow and gradual steps since a beginning was made on 1 August, 1946. Reduced fares, like all bargain prices, must inevitably result in an increase in demand, and neither the railways' manpower nor their rolling stock is sufficient as yet to meet any considerable increase.

For one popular relaxation we may, however, be thankful as a symbol and a portent of things to come. At 8.45 a.m. precisely on Tuesday, 15 August, 1946, the first post-war excursion train steamed out of Paddington. And what an excursion! It was the famous Kiddies' Express, heading for Weston-super-Mare, whose City Council entered joyfully into the scheme. The five hundred reserved seats were sold out long before the appointed day. Among the five hundred were a group of happy Paddington children who travelled as the guests of an unknown overseas visitor, Mr. J. Ellis Crofton, who by that time was on the high seas returning to Johannesburg.

CATERING

Before the war 110 Great Western trains included restaurant cars. About one in six of these were business trains on which restaurant facilities represented an important saving in time and effort to hard-worked people. The pressure of wartime traffic made it necessary for these facilities to be withdrawn; even at this date the Railway is compelled to proceed slowly with their reinstatement. The interest of the majority of travellers demands that restaurant cars should not be introduced at the expense of ordinary passenger accommodation. Additional cars, therefore, can only be brought back into circulation as and when increases are effected in the capacity of train services generally. The severity of the pressure on existing accommodation is shown by the fact that during the 1945 Christmas season the Government arranged for those railways that had already introduced restaurant cars to withdraw them again for a period of ten days. The Great Western was more cautious; its first restaurant car services did not reappear till 31 December, 1945, when the Christmas rush was over.

Much praise has been given to the meals in these cars. A three-course luncheon or dinner still costs only 3s. 6d. Breakfast and afternoon tea is provided *à la carte*. The few cars now running cannot hope to supply more than a small fraction of the demand, which is enormous. The cars are limited to single units (which may seat 50, 44 or 42 passengers according to the type of car), and in an endeavour to meet the demand for meals as far as possible, three and sometimes four sittings of luncheon and dinner are served, which is more than the kitchens were designed to provide. The traditional standards of Great Western service have successfully been maintained; but it is hard going for the men as well as for the equipment.

The restaurant car is a popular institution, and where the service is based on the set *table d'hôte* luncheon and dinner it has the great advantage of providing many substantial meals in a relatively short period of time. Nevertheless, there are inescapable drawbacks. A normal train of twelve coaches, when the space required for train staff, luggage and parcels has been allowed for, contains a net passenger accommodation equivalent to eleven coaches in all. It will be seen that a single restaurant car with seating capacity for 50 passengers involves a sacrifice of ten per cent. in the passenger accommodation of the train. Even with three sittings only a little more than one passenger in four can expect to be served with a meal. With a two-car unit the number of passengers who can be served approaches fifty per cent., but this increase is obtained at a high price, for the passenger accommodation is now reduced by nineteen per cent. instead of ten per cent.

THE BUFFET SERVICE

So that a larger proportion of passengers might take advantage of the catering service on trains, the Great Western nearly a quarter of a century ago introduced a type of car which has since been known as a buffet car. Being in the nature of an experiment, the first cars were not specially built for the job; old cars were converted so that by a process of trial and error the ideal design might gradually be evolved. The first full-length buffet cars in which the buffet (including pantry) occupies the entire length of the vehicle were built in 1934. These cars have a forty-foot counter with twelve stools. Another type of buffet car has eight stools at the counter and seating for twenty at tables. Composite cars in which a smaller buffet saloon takes up only half the total length have also proved exceedingly useful.

The latest type of train buffet, now still in the design stage, is being planned for the particular benefit of the very large group of travellers whose wants are limited to simple and inexpensive refreshment. This buffet, in the space of half a coach, would

15

provide a maximum of drinks and snacks at smallest possible cost in terms of train accommodation. It will be used either with or without a restaurant car on the same train, and should prove of special help to families with young and thirsty children.

In the early part of 1946, world-wide interest was created by the announcement that Great Western engineers were about to start work on the construction of an automatic buffet car, believed to be the first of its kind in the world. In this car, passengers will be able to purchase snacks, drinks and smokes by dropping sixpence or a shilling in the appropriate slot. There are stand-up counters for those who choose to consume their refreshments in the car, but the proportion of passengers wishing to carry theirs back to their compartments is expected to be higher than with the existing type of buffet car.

Behind these new developments lies the fact that a steady expansion is taking place in the public demand for meals and refreshments on trains. The Great Western is closely studying the trend of this movement, and new methods and devices are being introduced to meet each new situation as it occurs.

SLEEPERS

Great Western sleeper services have long been famous for their smooth riding, their quiet compartments, and their comfortable beds. There were eight daily Great Western trains with sleeping accommodation before the war, all with first and third class berths. The services were supplied by a fleet of 27 cars. In December, 1942, sleeping car facilities for all practical purposes ceased to be available to civilian travellers. A skeleton service for Government officials and others travelling on essential war work was, however, maintained. At the end of the war, ten sleeping cars were in operation on trains to Plymouth, Penzance, Neyland and Newquay.

On 17 September, 1945, the Government agreed to release a proportion amounting to rather more than half of the sleeper accommodation for the use of ordinary travellers. The proportion of freed accommodation has gradually been increased since that date. The hope has often been expressed that the necessity for reserving accommodation exclusively for Government officials may soon disappear. An early release is the more to be desired because it may be some time before the number of sleeping cars in service can be increased. A number of additional sleeping cars as well as restaurant cars are waiting to be reconditioned and refitted. If the materials were to be made available the work would not take long to complete. But under the conditions of pressure existing to-day, the Great Western does not feel justified in extending facilities for eating or sleeping at the expense of ordinary passenger accommodation. One day there will be more locomotives, more coaches and more trains. Meanwhile, its first business is transport. The Railway must go on.

CHAPTER TWO · THE FREIGHT SERVICE

STANDARDS OF EFFICIENCY

So quiet and unobtrusive are the freight services on a modern railway system that it may come as a surprise to some passengers to learn that Great Western freight trains represent a very substantial part of the total traffic movement on the Railway. In the year 1945, for example, out of the total mileage run by Great Western locomotives in an average week, 56 per cent. was concerned with freight and 44 per cent. with passengers. Without question, the carriage of freight is an essential public service in the fullest meaning of that term.

Reference is made in another chapter to the great work that is being done in the maintenance shops and to the programmes for new construction. Less spectacular but if possible of even higher significance is the steady progress in the restoration of pre-war standards of efficiency in the vital operations performed in freight yards, marshalling yards and sheds. During recent years, many goods stations have been extended and modernised and some have been so completely remodelled as to provide the equivalent of a brand new building.

The equipment in these stations is being constantly improved. To reduce shunting and handling operations to a minimum, various mechanical devices such as electric capstans, overhead large-capacity lifting equipment, mobile electric cranes, and self-propelled platform trucks have been installed. A comprehensive study of all developments in mechanical appliances and other equipment is made by a research committee of experts. The review which is at present taking place includes gravity roller runways and fork lift trucks for speedier handling of merchandise, pallets for the greater utilisation of existing storage accommodation, and a new type of container designed for the rapid discharge of various materials in bulk.

EXPRESS FREIGHT TRAINS

But the first and greatest need, once the war was over, was the restoration of the fast timetable trains for freight that are known as express freight trains. The operation of these trains is limited for the time being by the shortage of special rolling stock, since every express freight train requires a specified number of wagons to be equipped with

17

vacuum brakes controlled by the driver of the train. Thus, in the fastest freight trains the proportion of wagons having vacuum brakes may vary between one-third and one-half; such a train is allowed to travel at an average maximum speed of forty-five miles per hour. For trains with less than one-third vacuum brake wagons, the permissible speed is ten miles per hour less.

The post-war restoration of express vacuum fitted freight trains started with services between London and South Wales, followed after a short interval by trains between London and Bristol; between London, Birmingham, Shrewsbury and the North; between London, Gloucester and Worcester; between London and the West of England; and between the Midlands and Penzance. Sixty-eight of these trains were running again in 1945; at the end of 1946, a total of seventy-five express freight trains were in daily circulation. Additional trains can only be introduced when suitable loco-motives and vacuum brake wagons are brought into service.

In the long view, however, the development of express freight train services is conditioned less by the amount of rolling stock in circulation than by the available track capacity. It is therefore a matter of some importance to British industry and to the public generally that these services should be so planned that they may prove of the greatest practical benefit to those who need them most in the efficient pursuit of their business. This is the responsibility of a group of Great Western research workers who study the flow of traffic passing between different parts of the system, and estimate the probable requirements of the areas served. In this matter as in every other branch of its great business, it is the object of the management to reap all the advantages of centralised control, but to combine with them the intimate grasp of local conditions which can only be fully acquired through the untrammelled initiative of the man on the spot.

SPECIAL TRAFFICS

There are those who believe that a public service can only be fully efficient if it provides the same standardised facilities for all its users. The Great Western has never subscribed to this belief. Its philosophy since the earliest days has been governed by a strong sense of the value of flexibility. There is no achievement in which it takes greater pride than its ability to meet the individual requirements of the customer having a special and exceptional piece of work to do. Its object is to meet these requirements not only quickly and economically, which is important to this particular customer, but without detriment to the standard services, which is important to all the rest. Thus, on the passenger side, excursions of every type have been catered for, including a long series of educational excursions organised by schools. Often a single excursion has required a number of trains, in certain exceptional cases as many as thirty. Most of the difficult special jobs, however, relate to the transport of freight, and since the freight service seldom comes under the notice of the travelling public a few words upon the subject may not be out of place in this account.

A considerable proportion of the special freight traffics is due to seasonal and recurring movements in important fruit and vegetable crops such as spring cabbages, tomatoes, sugar beet, cider apples and plums. Where the volume to be handled is sufficient, special expresses are run. In the stress of war these facilities had perforce to be withdrawn, though there were, of course, notable exceptions. For example, early potato crops from Cornwall and Pembrokeshire replaced the Jersey crop from which the enemy had cut us off. Many special trains were run for these crops; those from Cornwall in particular ran long distances to meet shortages in the areas most acutely affected, such as the Midlands and the North. Yet it was a source of the keenest satisfaction to the men of the Great Western to see these services fully restored in the 1945 season, when a large number of express freight trains left the Worcester area laden with many kinds of fruit.

To people in London and other great cities, the flower expresses from Cornwall which ran again for the first time in April, 1946, brought the pleasantest of reminders that peace had indeed returned to this hard-pressed land. In that year's season, express freight trains carried for distribution throughout the country 175,000 tons of fruit and vegetables – broccoli and early potatoes from Cornwall, early pototoes from West Wales, plums, apples, beans, peas, brussels sprouts, asparagus, and other delicacies from the Vale of Evesham, and tomatoes from the Channel Islands (over four-and-a-half million packages from Guernsey and Jersey were handled at Weymouth). To ensure that these highly perishable goods reached the markets as soon after harvesting as possible, over a thousand special trains were run, not counting the fifteen special expresses which ran daily to distribute the plum crops of the short Worcester season. The 1946-7 sugar beet season involved the delivery of 205,000 tons of beets from various parts of the country to factories situated on the Great Western, and the collection of many more thousands of tons destined for factories elsewhere.

ET CIRCENSES

With all food cargoes, speed is the first essential. Many special installations have been planned with the object of saving every minute. At Smithfield, for example, the Railway has an underground goods station directly underneath the Central Meat Market. Meat and offal from the Birkenhead abattoirs and the West of England arriving at this station at the rate of more than one hundred tons a day are unloaded in the early morning and go straight up to the market stalls in lifts. It has been mentioned that most of these special traffics are recurring so that plans can be made some time in advance; but sudden demands are not infrequent. Here is a typical case. In 1946, a ship carrying 1,600 tons of grapefruit bound for a north-eastern port developed engine trouble and put in to Plymouth. At very short warning, the Railway provided five special trains which enabled the precious cargo to reach its destination before the appointed time.

The carriage of refrigerated food is a highly specialised business. After years of research the Great Western is now able to offer a service which can be relied upon to preserve the initial temperature of the cargo, whatever that may be. By the use of insulated containers, goods which have to be taken by road vehicle from (or to) stores or markets can be conveyed without a break in refrigeration. In this way, for example, 1,830 tons of ice cream were carried in perfect condition in the year 1946.

It will be gathered from these particulars that the carriage of every kind of food must necessarily take an important place in the planning of the freight trains of the future. The reasons for this emphasis are clear enough. The Railway is privileged to serve some of the finest food-producing regions of Britain. Its position as a carrier of essential foods is unique. It is the policy of the management that the quality of its food distribution service must be worthy of this great position. Seven lean years have left the people of this country weary of the drab monotony of wartime meals. In such relief as has already taken place, the Railway has been able to play a useful part. But a great deal more remains to be accomplished before the workers in essential industries enjoy the full variety of fresh food to which they have been accustomed. As and when better supplies become available, the Great Western food distribution services will be ready to handle them more swiftly than ever before, providing for every type of food whatever special conditions may be most effective in keeping it immaculately fresh.

Yet however important the food services may be, they do not constitute the whole of the special traffics for which provision must be made. There is, for example, the carriage of live animals. This is a kind of business in which the Great Western has had much experience. Cattle from Ireland, animals from marts, fairs and sales, flocks of sheep travelling between winter and summer pastures, are dealt with in considerable volume. Before the war, there was a constant movement of racehorses, circus animals and cattle for agricultural shows.

Perhaps the most interesting loads are those consisting of out-of-gauge units such as large machinery and plant. There is a big stock of specially designed wagons to deal with these. In certain cases ingenious tools and gear may have to be employed, as for example with locomotives and rolling stock built for railways abroad, which are often considerably larger than those used on British railways. When these are conveyed by train in this country, various types of traversing gear are provided to enable them to travel safely past bridges, station platforms and the like.

THE TRAVELLING POST OFFICE

While for the greater bulk of its traffics the Great Western is not called upon to do more than act as a railway carrier transporting a cargo from one place to another,

THE TRAVELLING POST OFFICE

there are cases where services of quite a different order are asked for. The Railway, for example, will warehouse goods, dismantle and erect machinery, decant liquids, water cattle, and perform many other duties in relation to the freight, animate or inanimate, that goes on its trains. The list of firms that regularly avail themselves of these facilities includes some of the best-known names in the country. Of all the examples of special services organised for an important customer perhaps the most interesting is the mobile workshop commonly referred to as the Travelling Post Office.

A mobile sorting office containing staff at work should not perhaps be dealt with under the heading of freight, but as an example of flexibility in meeting special demands the Travelling Post Office is of unusual interest. The association between the Great Western and the General Post Office has always been an intimate one. The Railway was the first to introduce a fully equipped Crown Post Office in one of its stations. This was the Paddington Station Branch Office, opened by Sir Kingsley Wood on 22 May, 1935. Eighty years earlier, on 1 February, 1855, the first Postal Train in the world had started service between London and Bristol. The train, consisting of two sorting carriages and a van, was drawn by one of the old seven-foot single engines. It was not the first travelling post office, for sorting carriages in which the work of the Post Office was carried on first came into use in 1841, but it was the first to have a train all to itself. The Postal Train in this exclusive sense was in abeyance for thirty-two years between 1870 and 1902, and more recently suffered another eclipse from 1940 onwards. Its restoration on the Paddington to Penzance run, which took place on Monday, 1 October, 1945, was an occasion for official rejoicing.

The two sorting carriages and one van of 1855 have now expanded into three carriages and seven vans, and there have been a number of incidental improvements. One of the earliest was the ingenious appliance for depositing and picking up mails without stopping which was first installed in 1866, with stationary apparatus established at Slough and Maidenhead. The appliance, which is familiar to every schoolboy, includes a stout leather mail pouch which is suspended from a hook swung out from the side of the train and at the appropriate point picked up in a stationary net; or vice versa. This apparatus is now used at Liskeard on the up journey, and at Maidenhead, Swindon, Chippenham and Liskeard going down. The bulk of the mail is, of course, handled in the usual way at the regular stopping points which include Bristol, Exeter and Plymouth. There is one train in both directions. Each train travels through the night, the up train starting at 6.40 p.m. and the down train at 10.10 p.m.

ROAD AND RAIL

The railway freight service in this country, unlike the public passenger service, has for many years offered its customers through transport from door-to-door at all-in rates. To-day, a considerable number of the freight consignments handled by the Great

THE FREIGHT SERVICE

Western includes transport by road as well as by rail as an integral part of the service. A comprehensive service of this kind brings many new responsibilities. However fast and reliable the train service may be, the needs of the customer for freight transport will not be adequately met unless at each end of the journey the road services for collection and distribution, and the arrangements for transferring the freight from one vehicle to another, are of the same high quality as the services from station to station on the line.

For some years past, the Great Western, under a joint arrangement with the other railway companies, has made a close study of the problems associated with terminal services linking railway stations with the premises of senders and consignees. The results of these investigations are now being applied on an ever-widening scale. A measure of the efficiency of the road motor services will be found in the simple fact that in the year 1945 the fleet of lorries carried 18 per cent. more goods (measured by weight) than in the last year before the war, despite the fact that motor units travelled 4½ million fewer miles (a reduction of 21 per cent.). This considerable gain in the volume of work done per vehicle-mile was effected through a general reorganisation, which included the use of modern vehicles of greater capacity. The result, of course, was a very substantial saving in wear and tear as well as fuel.

The increase in efficiency achieved was actually greater than the figure of 18 per cent. would suggest. During 1945 the proportion of the total fleet of motor vehicles withdrawn for repairs was almost exactly 50 per cent. greater than in 1938. These abnormal repairs were a direct result of wartime wear and tear, and of the enforced postponement of maintenance work and renewals. A policy of "make do and mend" was inevitable.

The reduction in the size of the effective fleet of vehicles was a grievous handicap which is still continuing at the time of writing. There is only one way of surmounting this handicap, and that is to pursue with the greatest energy the replacement of old vehicles with new until the pre-war age limit is once more in effective operation. Existing Government priorities for the commercial motor industry make this task especially difficult at the present time. Progress in overcoming the serious arrears of renewals has been disappointing. At the close of November, 1946, out of seven hundred motor vehicles and trailers ordered for delivery during 1946, 129 motor vehicles and five trailers only had been delivered. (This figure does not include the considerable arrears on the 1945 programme delivered in the following year).

PLANNED DISTRIBUTION

In the very early days, the railways had to rely upon their own horse transport supplemented by the employment of many local hauliers who, through the terms of their agreements, became an integral part of railway organisation. With the development of the internal combustion engine, the number of horses rapidly diminished and motor transport took their place. Country areas far away from the railway could now be easily and quickly connected by road, and what was known as the Country Lorry Service was instituted to provide this connection. This service, which first took motor transport for railborne goods beyond the usual collection and delivery radius, roughly coincident with that of the built-up urban area and its immediate fringe, soon proved of special value to the farmers of Cornwall and Western Wales. Its convenience and simplicity are not the least of its attractions. The frequency of the service to a particular area is governed by the volume of traffic offering, but daily deliveries are generally aimed at. For traders with regular flows of traffic for delivery over a wide area, the Railway will quote special terms covering special services such as the decanting of liquids from drums and the collection of empties. The customer's costing is greatly facilitated by the fixing of such inclusive charges, which may be worked out at so much per gallon or per unit of weight.

Another striking example of efficient goods distribution is the specialised Railhead Delivery Service planned to meet the needs of the retail distributive trades. Road vehicles attached to this Service operate daily from Reading, Birmingham, Bristol, Exeter, Newport, Cardiff and Swansea over a distance of roundly thirty miles from the city centre. Goods may be sent in bulk for breaking down and sorting upon arrival and for delivery in accordance with the sender's instructions. The saving in labour and material for packing is obvious. Traders may arrange to have credit notes issued for empties which are collected and returned. Those who wish their firms to be directly associated with the road delivery of their goods may have Great Western motor vans painted in their own colours and adorned with their names.

At a number of strategically situated stations fully-equipped warehouses may be leased wholly or in part according to each trader's needs. This arrangement enables a manufacturer or merchant to forward his goods in bulk to a railway goods station (usually in a thickly-populated area) to be stored there for despatch as and when required. The trader may provide his own staff to superintend the warehousing and keep the records; or if he wishes it the Railway will perform these services for him. If a specialised Railhead Delivery Service operates from the particular station at which a trader has a warehouse, he may, of course (unless he has a fleet of vehicles of his own) make use of this service; if not, the Railway will arrange distribution through its normal service by rail or road.

THE SMALL CONSIGNMENT

In some respects the most important of the Great Western's combined rail and road operations is the service for the carriage of small consignments. That, no doubt. is the reason why among the post-war improvements planned by the Railway, the reorganisation of "smalls" traffic plays such a conspicuous part.

Where, for one reason or another, it is necessary that delivery should take place on the same day on which the goods are despatched, the passenger train service provides the best solution. Passenger trains also carry the class of traffic handled under the the designation of "parcels." But goods traffic requiring this maximum speed is exceptional. Moreover, the capacity of the passenger train service is limited, and the cost of this form of transport must always be relatively high. The majority of customers with "smalls" traffic are content with a twenty-four hour service, which can be provided more economically at freight traffic rates.

Radical improvements have been instituted from time to time for the purpose of accelerating the movement of "smalls." The Country Lorry Service was one of these. In addition, methods of handling and sorting have been constantly reviewed and brought up to date, goods sheds have been replanned and extended, the number of express freight trains has been increased, and road transport has been used to by-pass some of the operations. Before the war, a point had been reached where approximately 70 per cent. of small consignments reached their destinations the day after they were sent. The Great Western is now perfecting a new scheme which should ultimately ensure next-day delivery in all parts of its system. At the moment of writing the scheme is in operation in many important areas, including the Midlands; the whole of Great Western local traffic is expected to be covered by the early summer of 1947. While its full benefits can only be achieved when it is universally applied throughout the entire railway network of this country, most satisfactory results are already being achieved.

The main object of this system, known as the zonal collection and delivery system, is to avoid or reduce what is called the transhipment of goods, that is to say their transfer from one railway wagon to another at some stage of their journey. Every such transhipment takes not less than a day and often more. The more stations are used to serve a given area, the smaller will be the volume of goods to be despatched to each station, and, by the same token, the more transhipments will be necessary to get them there. The zonal system is, in its essence, a device for reducing the need for transhipment by using fewer stations and making each station handle a greater load of goods.

The system was planned early in 1944, when the Great Western, mindful of its peacetime obligations, undertook a comprehensive review of "smalls" traffic in all parts of its territory. The next step was the creation of thirty-six areas (the figure at the moment of writing is not quite final), each served by a central station (the railhead) linked with a small number of subsidiary stations (the sub-railheads). The necessary volume of traffic at sub-railheads is obtained by arranging for each sub-railhead to serve an area previously covered by three or four stations. To ensure the greatest speed of communication, goods that cannot be made up into direct wagons at the sub-railhead are carried in both directions by road or, where suitable services exist, by passenger train. The road motor services between the railhead and the sub-railhead run to a time-table related to that of the fast freight trains.

THE BIRMINGHAM EXPERIMENT

The first of the zones to be established, that which covers the neighbourhood of Birmingham, provides a useful illustration of the service which the Railway is now gradually bringing to completion. The area served from the Birmingham railhead is roundly 160 miles in extent, and runs from Erdington and Great Bridge in the north to Lapworth in the south. To-day, the "smalls" traffic which used to be handled at twenty stations and three subsidiary depots (twenty-three centres in all) is concentrated at five stations, improved and reorganised as befits their new function.

The zonal system for small consignments was inaugurated at Birmingham on 3 December, 1945. Its success after some months of operation caused the time schedule for other areas to be considerably advanced. No less than ten additional railheads were established during the summer of 1946. The Cardiff zone came into operation under the new plan on 1 July, with Pontypridd and Port Talbot a month later. Progress maps illustrating the evolution of these zones will be found at the end of this book. Worcester and Redruth also followed on 1 August, Reading, Leamington, Wolverhampton, Swindon and St. Austell on 1 October, Newport, Plymouth and Trowbridge on 1 December, and Bristol and Slough on 1 January, 1947. The Swindon zone is the largest of these. Its area of one thousand square miles formerly had forty-four stations handling small consignments; six sub-railheads have now taken over this work.

The greater volume of traffic now handled at the sub-railheads means that more direct wagons can travel without transhipment. The saving of time may often be considerable. More time is saved by the increased use of road transport; the extent of this increase may be gathered from the fact that in the Birmingham district alone the additional road mileage required for the new improved service is estimated to be in the region of 110,000 miles a year. If the rapid transport of small consignments has long been a difficult problem, it is largely because no complete solution is offered by either rail or road transport used alone. The combination of the two in a single system of door-to-door transport has provided what for many years to come will be regarded as the best attainable answer. But something more is required than efficiency in each of the two forms of transport. If the customer is to get the utmost benefit from the combination, the work of both branches must be planned as a whole so that each is made to contribute according to its capacity to the best total result.

CHAPTER THREE · LOCOMOTIVES

PROBLEMS OF MOTIVE POWER

I⊤ is no accident that the Great Western should have achieved a world-wide reputation as a builder of locomotives. Its remarkable train services could never have been developed without high-powered engines of advanced and super-efficient design. Constantly through the Railway's history, new standards of speed and endurance set by the operating chiefs stimulated the engineers to even greater exertions. One such challenge was the epoch-making run from Paddington to Plymouth in 1903, made without a stop at an average speed of 63·4 miles per hour from start to finish. So that speed might be maintained over the sharp gradients west of Newton Abbot, the run was made with a train of five coaches only. A regular non-stop service meant longer trains as well as greater reserves of power. And so from that bold challenge there sprung those powerful new locomotives having six coupled driving wheels which were later standardised in the famous *Castle* and *King* classes. The *King* locomotives, incidentally, are still the most powerful 4-6-0 passenger engines we have in this country. The Great Western has never been content to stand still, least of all in the pursuit of high locomotive performance.

To-day the pursuit continues, though the aims to be achieved are not quite the same. While West Country trains still have to negotiate some of the steepest gradients in the British Isles, it is generally true to say that the length and speed of trains have reached a point beyond which they cannot advance very far without extensive reconstruction of tracks, bridges and stations. Emphasis has therefore shifted to other properties than mere power. Economy in labour and fuel, flexibility in operation, absolute reliability under varying conditions of service, these are some of the objects to which the modern designer is expected to give first attention. New materials and new fuels offer opportunities that his predecessors could not have imagined. The crux of the problem is the way in which fuel is transformed into instantly available motive power. Of all the solutions now under investigation, the most revolutionary is the development of engines in which power is no longer transmitted through pistons sliding to and fro. On 6 March, 1946, Viscount Portal, Chairman of the Great Western, announced that the Railway had under consideration plans for the construction of gas turbine loco-

27

motives. True to its century-old tradition of technical leadership, the Great Western once again was early in the field.

NEW CONSTRUCTION

For the moment, however, the restoration of 1939 standards of service is the overriding need. This account must therefore consider first the immediate plans for strengthening the locomotive fleet. The Great Western estimates that to overtake arrears of renewals and to continue the work of current renewal at its appropriate rate, seven hundred new locomotives will be needed in the five-year period from 1946 to 1950. The programme for the two years 1946 and 1947 provides for the building of 220 new locomotives, roundly, 110 in each year. Many types are represented, but more than half of the new locomotives are passenger engines, mainly of the *Castle* and the new *County* classes, though passenger tank engines also are being built. It is regrettable that the target for 1946 was not reached; but even if it had been, new building would barely have equalled replacements. The net result was similar to that for 1945, when eighty new locomotives were produced against a withdrawal of ninety, leaving a net loss of ten locomotives at the end of the year. It so happens, however, that during the war the fleet of goods locomotives was strengthened in relation to the passenger locomotive fleet, so that the works are now able to concentrate their energies on new passenger locomotives. Despite the fact, therefore, that the total locomotive fleet remained stationary, the number of passenger locomotives was somewhat greater by the end of 1946. It is unnecessary to stress the importance of this improvement to those who are responsible for building up the passenger train service.

Further progress will necessarily be slow. As production increases, so the number of withdrawals must also be increased. There is an excessive number of old locomotives still to be weeded out. At the end of 1946, 546 locomotives over forty years old were in daily service as compared with 450 in 1938, an increase of 21 per cent.

TECHNICAL DEVELOPMENT

As a matter of course, the new locomotives will incorporate a number of special devices which have been developed by the Swindon research department from time to time. In some cases these devices are being re-examined with a view to further improvement or simplification. A typical example is the steam superheating apparatus which, like so many other devices, was originally introduced into this country by the Great Western. The use of superheated steam, i.e., of steam heated to a temperature of about 600 degrees Fahrenheit – causes a substantial rise in power output, largely by increasing the amount of steam delivered to the cylinders and reducing the loss of steam within the cylinders due to condensation. It is forty-one years – it was in April 1906 to be precise – since there came out of the Swindon works the first locomotive to

A COUNTY CLASS LOCOMOTIVE

UNDER TEST AT SWINDON

be equipped with this type of apparatus. An improved design was afterwards adopted as standard for all the Railway's locomotives except those used for shunting.

It is worth mentioning here how much is owed in the development of new Great Western locomotives to the vision and courage of the management which in the year 1904 constructed a locomotive testing plant which is still the only one of its kind in this country, though a second plant is now projected elsewhere. The purpose of this plant is to enable tests to be made under more constant conditions than those normally obtaining on the track. When a locomotive is to be tested, it is anchored with all its wheels resting on great rollers turning in water-cooled bearings. The bearings are housed in sliding carriages moved into position by an electric motor. Elaborate recording equipment is installed at a large number of points so that observations may be made of engine speed, cylinder pressure and temperatures, smoke-box vacua and temperatures, the quantities of coal and water consumed, the calorific value and chemical composition of the coal, and the chemical content of the products of combustion.

Just before the war, the capacity of the plant was increased and the equipment generally improved; every current type of Great Western locomotive can now be tested to its full power as developed under average conditions of working.

THE COUNTY CLASS

Among the new locomotive designs is an improved version of the well-known *Hall* class. This is the *County* class whose serial numbers begin with 1,000. An important characteristic of this locomotive is the higher boiler pressure. It will be recalled that during the first quarter of the present century the Great Western consistently led the way in the use of higher pressures. There has, however, been no further increase since 1927, when the first appearance of the *King* class startled and delighted the railway world. The new *County* class is one of the two new types of locomotives now in use in this country in which the steam pressure is increased by a further 12 per cent. to 280 lbs. per square inch, as compared to 250 lbs. in the *King* class. Other improvements include a larger capacity superheater giving a higher degree of superheat. Externally, the new locomotives may be easily distinguished by the straight continuous splasher which replaces the three separate splashers over the driving wheels. Thirty *County* class locomotives are to be built in 1946-47.

An entirely new departure in Great Western locomotive design is included in the experimental *County* class locomotive No. 1,000. This locomotive is equipped with two blast pipes, and its outward appearance is distinguished by a broad chimney elliptical instead of circular in section. A view of this locomotive appears on page 32.

OIL BURNING LOCOMOTIVES

In its pursuit of greater efficiency and economy, the Great Western started towards the end of the war upon a series of experiments with permanent oil burning equipment for ordinary steam locomotives. The experiments were confined to existing locomotives; no new steam locomotives specially designed for oil burning are at the moment being planned. The use of oil fuel is being investigated for several reasons. First, it is clear that there must be some saving in time and labour in the servicing and preparation of such locomotives, though the precise extent of the saving can only be determined by experience. There is also the fact that coal of good quality having the necessary steam-producing capacity is in short supply, and there is little prospect of an early improvement in deliveries. Arrangements were therefore made in 1945 for a small number of locomotives to be converted from coal to oil. The tenders were to carry a 1,800 gallon oil tank with a feed pipe running to the oil burning apparatus on the locomotive. These 1,800 gallons go a long way. Refuelling depots, each of 36,000 gallon capacity, were established at Llanelly and Severn Tunnel Junction.

At the end of 1945, four 2-8-0 oil burning locomotives had been in service for some months. Everyone agreed that the experiment had been more than justified in the result. A heavy locomotive under load consumes about 6½ gallons of heavy fuel oil per mile (as compared with 72 lbs. of coal). The use of oil, moreover, enabled savings to be effected in servicing while the engines are in the running sheds; much labour was saved by the elimination of coal loading and ash removal. The work of the fireman on the footplate was also considerably reduced. The trial locomotives had proved themselves capable of taking the full maximum load and the consumption of fuel oil was less than was anticipated. Their performance on the track as well as their greater cleanliness and ease of handling had won enthusiastic approval from the footplate crews. The process of conversion was simple. If the price of oil fuel were to show a substantial drop in relation to the cost of coal, it would be perfectly feasible for one or more locomotive sheds with their entire fleets to be changed over from coal to oil fuel.

Meanwhile, arrangements were made at once to convert eighteen heavy freight locomotives. By the summer of 1946, ten of these were in service in South Wales where they were regularly used to draw coal and freight trains each weighing up to one thousand tons.

As a result of the experiments and in view of the continued shortage of coal (supplies of oil being assured) it was decided to extend the experiment to passenger services, and at 9.0 a.m. on Friday, 18 October, engine No. 5091 of the *Castle* class left Swindon as an oil burning locomotive to work express passenger trains between Paddington and Bristol, commencing with the 1.18 p.m. train from Paddington.

In August, 1946, the Government, impressed with the success of these experiments, announced the forthcoming conversion of twelve hundred British railway locomotives to oil firing. The Great Western's experience with its oil burners had been so satisfactory that its original designs for locomotive equipment and oil storage installations

LOCOMOTIVE NO. 1,000

THE COUNTY OF MIDDLESEX

were used as the basis for the entire scheme. Many of the Railway's standard components were also adopted as standard for British railways generally.

On the Great Western system, fourteen new installations will be provided at Old Oak Common, Reading, Didcot, Banbury, Swindon, Westbury, Gloucester, Bristol (Bath Road), Bristol (St. Phillips Marsh), Newton Abbot, Plymouth (Laira), Newport (Ebbw Junction), Cardiff (Canton), and Swansea (Landore). With the existing installations at Llanelly and Severn Tunnel Junction, they will handle 125,000 gallons of oil on an average day and will have an aggregate storage capacity of about two million gallons – roundly fourteen days' supply. 184 locomotives – twenty-five of the *Castle* class, seventy-three heavy 2-8-0 freight engines, and eighty-six mixed traffic engines, mostly of the 4-6-0 type, will run on oil fuel. It is estimated that under the Great Western scheme alone some 173,000 tons of coal a year will be saved.

RAILCARS

It is well known that the Great Western has led all British railways in the use of the modern railcar, the automotive vehicle which combines the function of a locomotive with that of a passenger carriage. The history books show that this lead was first established nearly a century ago. It was in 1848 that the Bristol and Exeter Company (an undertaking absorbed by the Great Western twenty-eight years later) designed and built the railcar *Fairfield*, with accommodation for forty-eight passengers. The *Fairfield*, the first railcar in the world, was a hybrid vehicle with a boiler and engine of traditional shape at the fore end. This bold experiment was ahead of its time; it was not till 1903 that the Great Western was able to inaugurate a planned railcar service between Stonehouse and Chalford in the Stroud Valley. The vehicles this time were of the true railcar type, with a steam engine built into a continuous carriage body. "I believe," Lord Cawdor, the then Chairman, told the shareholders, "there is a considerable future for motor cars on rails." His confidence was justified. There was.

The Diesel-engined vehicles, which are the modern successors of those early railcars, have been much praised for their rapid yet smooth acceleration and their quiet riding at full speed. People who live on or near the routes over which they run are familiar with the Great Western warning signal (also standard on French railcars). These railcars were first introduced for the purpose of providing improved services at points where traffic is not sufficiently heavy to justify the running of full-length steam trains at short intervals. It was anticipated that the cars would be used during the development period only, and that they would be succeeded by steam trains as traffic increased. Their success, however, exceeded all expectations. There followed, in rapid succession, bigger, higher-powered cars with buffet and lavatory facilities, smaller cars for hauling one or two horse-boxes or other special traffic on branch lines, and other types of car to convey parcels traffic only.

THE FIRST OIL BURNING

PASSENGER LOCOMOTIVE

The first Diesel railcar service was introduced on 4 December, 1933. It was run by a single car which covered a total of 1,374 miles a week to provide additional transport between Southall, Slough, Reading, Didcot and Oxford, and which was also used, except on Saturdays, on a trip from Reading to Henley. The larger cars with buffet facilities first ran on 9 July, 1934, between Birmingham and Cardiff, a distance of 117 miles. A supplement of 2/6 was charged in addition to the third-class fare, but this was abolished a year later. In October in the same year an additional stop was included at Cheltenham Spa (Malvern Road); this meant an extra minute on the journey time from Birmingham to Cardiff for the next nine months, after which the original journey time was reinstated.

On 8 July, 1935, new Diesel railcar services (without buffet facilities) were introduced between Oxford and Princes Risborough; Oxford and Didcot; Oxford, Kingham, Worcester and Hereford; Malvern Wells, Worcester and Birmingham; and Birmingham, Henley-in-Arden, Stratford on-Avon and Broadway. Early in 1936, more railcars came into service in the Oxford and Worcester districts, and also (Mondays to Fridays) between Bristol, Yeovil and Weymouth; Bristol and Salisbury; Yeovil and Taunton; Pontypool, Monmouth, Chepstow and Newport; Swansea, Port Talbot, Llanelly, Carmarthen and Whitland; and between Birmingham, Hatton and Stratford-on-Avon. The London district parcels car service was also inaugurated at this time. Later in the same year came services between Weston-super-Mare, Bristol and Cardiff, providing additional fast business services between Bristol and South Wales, and between Swansea, Morriston and Felin Fran.

At the end of the recent war, twenty-four cars (including two twin sets) out of a total of thirty-eight vehicles, were providing regular services totalling 3,562 miles each weekday; on Sundays, three cars ran a total of 333 miles. In the summer of 1946, the weekday total reached 4,385 miles. On 7 October, the buffet railcars which started the Birmingham-Cardiff service in July, 1934, were brought into use on Mondays to Fridays between Swansea, Cardiff, Newport and Gloucester. The new facility was much appreciated by business travellers between these important centres.

ENGINES FOR SHUNTING

The immediate programme for the next two years does not contemplate any increase in the Great Western's fleet of railcars. The new Diesel-electric locomotives included in the programme are vehicles of quite a different type. They are small locomotives specially designed for shunting. It is one of the drawbacks of coal-burning steam locomotives that they have to be stopped at intervals of not more than twenty-four hours to take in new supplies of coal and water, to have their fireboxes cleaned out and to receive attention generally. This limitation measurably reduces their efficiency in shunting work, which in many yards goes on continually for periods of six days or longer. After a careful study of alternative types of locomotives, the Great Western has selected the Diesel electric locomotives as the most suitable for shunting. Seven such locomotives are under construction and orders for more are to follow. They are being built at the Swindon locomotive works with power units supplied by two specialist firms.

The new locomotives will be able to work continuously for periods up to one week without refilling of the fuel tank. Another great advantage is that unlike the steam locomotive, which has to keep up steam when it is standing still, they burn fuel only when they are working, and in amounts corresponding closely with the amount of work performed. In the intermittent movement of the shunting yard, the unproductive use of fuel needs to be watched with special care, and the introduction of Diesel-electric locomotives should lead to a substantial saving in fuel costs and, what is even more important just now, in fuel, most precious of modern commodities.

STREAMLINING

This chapter so far has dealt with strictly technical matters. What about the appearance of the new locomotives? Will they be streamlined in accordance with the well-known American practice? Will they dazzle the eye with the brightness of polished aluminium or stainless steel?

It is necessary in an account of this kind that a word or two at least should be said about streamlining. As every schoolboy knows, if a vehicle is designed in accordance with certain established principles of aerodynamics, the air through which the vehicle passes will offer a minimum of resistance to its forward movement. The lessened resistance is, of course, most noticeable at high speeds, but it is a debatable point whether at the speed of an ordinary express train it is sufficient to result in a measurable saving of fuel. The Great Western started many years before the war to investigate the possibilities of streamlining. At the end of 1933, an experimental streamlined railcar was put into service between Southall and Didcot. A little later, two coal-burning steam locomotives – the *Manorbier Castle* and the *King Henry VII* – were fitted with improvised streamlined casings so that their efficiency might be tested under normal running conditions.

The result of these investigations was decisive. The streamlined railcar came to stay. The original design was developed in the new cars introduced for the service between Birmingham and South Wales in the following year. To-day, the streamlining of railcars is standard Great Western practice. The streamlining of steam locomotives is not.

The reasons for these decisions are many, and some of them are highly involved. But most of all the decisions rested on a consideration of the overall length of the trains concerned. The railcar body is sixty-two feet long. The full-length steam train is between nine hundred and one thousand feet long in all. The difference of length is important,

A DIESEL-MECHANICAL RAILCAR SET

END VIEW

because a vehicle running on rails has to overcome not only the head resistance applied to the front end, but also the less obvious effect of a sideways wind. In the railcar, head-wind resistance is a factor to be taken seriously; in the steam train it is negligible in proportion to the side thrust. The Great Western has always been an intensely practical railway. A streamlined locomotive might be good to look at, but the train went no faster because of it and the coal bill remained the same.

THE GAS TURBINE

But what of the new, revolutionary inventions demanding new visual expression? The harnessing of the gas turbine to railway operation is one of these. The turbine as a power unit is already familiar to railway engineers in the older form in which steam is used. It is many years ago now since the Great Western started to examine the possibilities of the locomotive driven by steam turbine power. Their conclusions were not unduly optimistic. The steam turbine at first glance has many advantages as a power unit. Certain types are remarkably economical to run. On the other side of the account are many difficulties and limitations which no designer has as yet succeeded in overcoming. Experimental steam turbine locomotives have been developed by a number of railway undertakings in all parts of the world, including one of the British

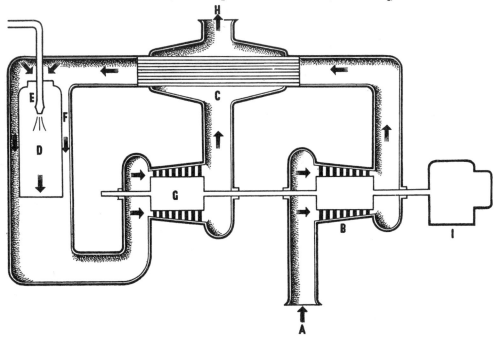

THE GAS TURBINE : SECTIONAL DIAGRAM

A GREAT WESTERN GAS TURBINE LOCOMOTIVE

PRELIMINARY DESIGN, 1946

companies, but none of these undertakings so far has thought it worth while to build additional locomotives to the same design. This fact is sufficient indication of the difficulty of adapting the steam turbine to the requirements of modern railway operation.

The principle of the gas turbine has been fairly widely known for some time, but its full development was delayed until metallurgical science could produce materials capable of working at a temperature of over 1,000 degrees Fahrenheit. The complete gas turbine unit (see the diagram on page 38) consists of four parts: the air compressor (B), the pre-heater (C), the combustion chamber (D) and, finally, the turbine itself (G). The air enters at A and, after being compressed and pre-heated, divides into two streams, one of which enters the combustion chamber (D) while the other by-passes the chamber at F – F. This by-pass air supply helps to ensure that the gas mixture which reaches the turbine is kept at the correct working temperature. The oil or other suitable fuel is injected through the burner (E). In the combustion chamber the pressure set up by the compressor is multiplied many times over by the expansion of the air in the intense heat, and further increased by the generation of combustion gases. After passing through the turbine, the hot gas mixture is used in the pre-heater to heat the incoming air and is then exhausted into the atmosphere at H. The main function of the turbine (which also drives the air compressor) is to drive the electric generator (I) from which current is supplied to the electric motors driving the locomotive. The turbine unit is started up by a starting motor which turns over the compressor, the fuel being ignited at the same time with an electric ignition rod. The whole unit is controlled from the driver's cab.

The two gas turbine locomotives which are now being built will develop a power output equal to 2,500 h.p. and will travel at a maximum speed of ninety miles an hour. The Great Western is determined to press forward the completion of these locomotives because it sees the possibility of a brilliant future for the new method of propulsion. One reason for this belief is that the output of power, both in relation to the weight of the engine and in relation to the fuel consumed, compares very favourably with that of the traditional piston engine. Another reason is that when sufficient experience has been gathered it should be possible to build turbine locomotives requiring only a small fraction of the maintenance work inevitably associated with steam locomotives of the traditional type.

Yet a further reason for the Railway's preoccupation is a more interesting one. The Great Western intends to maintain its position of leadership in the application of new forms of energy to railway traction. In a long view, it is possible that the gas turbine locomotive may prove to have been chiefly significant as the forerunner of even greater and more exciting Great Western locomotives to come.

CHAPTER FOUR · TRAINS

_____

THE RETURN TO NORMAL

Travel on the Great Western has always been surrounded with those little comforts and amenities that make it something more than a mere journey from one place to another. The standard in such matters as the heating, lighting and cleaning of compartments has been consistently high. The pre-war quality of passenger services will have been fully restored only when the setbacks suffered in these essential details are successfully overcome on every part of the system.

The heating of steam trains, as is well known, is done by means of steam from the locomotive. Its efficiency depends on two things, the best equipment and the best maintenance. Great Western equipment is good, but the war has seriously interfered with maintenance. Arrears of maintenance work on coaches has been piling up; here, as in most other departments, they are equivalent to some eighteen months of full-time work. Hundreds of coaches that by pre-war standards would have been taken out of service are kept at work so that the trains may run.

With steam heating there are also the troubles arising from inferior quality coal. At the best, poor quality coal will accentuate the effects of unskilled stoking, since the worse the coal the greater the volume that must be delivered to the fires; at the worst it may bring not only the heating but the train itself to a standstill. With trains of abnormal length, loss of steam pressure will affect the heating of the rear part very quickly.

These facts are given not by way of extenuation or excuse; they illustrate a state of affairs that probably affects Great Western employees even more than it does their passengers. The momentary discomfort soon passes; a diminution of public confidence and approval is a more serious matter. Daily the men and women of this Railway have fresh cause to realise that the necessity for using imperfect equipment and material in the performance of their work is not the least of the hardships that the war has brought upon them. They are determined to bring this equipment back to the customary standard of excellence and, where possible, to raise the standard even higher. There is, for example, a new type of heating installation that heats the rear part of a train more quickly and more effectively than the pre-war design, so that the loss of steam pressure will not leave passengers in the last two or three coaches to shiver. This new apparatus has been experimentally fitted on a small number of trains, and it is intended to make it universal as soon as the necessary materials become available.

On the subject of cleanliness in trains, the Great Western has been regarded as something of a fanatic. Its trains are held in special affection because of their relative freedom from soot and dirt; but soot is only one of many enemies of cleanliness, and the arrears of cleaning work which have accumulated during the war have presented the coach cleaning staff with a formidable problem. If their work is too thorough, progress will be slow, and much time will elapse before the whole of the fleet can be dealt with. Great Western men are not usually given to compromise, but in this case a compromise has been forced on them. None the less the 1939 standard of cleanliness is gradually being recaptured; the principal exception for the time being are the coaches scheduled for extensive repair work in 1948 or 1949.

The pre-war standard of lighting in coaches has now been restored in the bulk of the rolling stock. As with the heating, however, difficulties are still being caused by defective equipment. These difficulties will disappear as coaches are being dealt with in the repair shops. It will also have been noticed that there is a certain type of passenger who cannot resist the temptation to take away fittings and fixtures from railway coaches as souvenirs. The practice has resulted in a great many lampholders being found without lamps. Day by day the Railway is doing its best to keep up with the depredations, but the work is still several thousand lamps behind.

PASSENGER COACHES

To maintain a passenger train service of the high standard associated with the Great Western, it is necessary that a sufficient number of coaches should be available at all times. In a sense, the need for coaches is even more fundamental than the need for locomotives. If locomotives are lacking, it is always possible to use each one to the utmost of its capacity by running longer trains, as was done during the war. The trains will be there, though they will be more difficult to handle and therefore less fast. But where there are no coaches there can be no trains of any sort. The capacity to carry passengers is determined absolutely by the number of coaches a railway has available.

The situation to-day may be very clearly set forth by quoting some simple figures. In the summer of 1938, the Railway's total stock of coaches stood at 6,168, of which 5,819 were regularly available for service. The figures for the same period in 1946 were 5,738 and 4,441 respectively. The loss of coaches in daily service amounts to no less than 22.6 per cent. The figure, at the time of writing, is still rising. The increase in the number under repair is, of course, a natural consequence of war conditions. Repairs during the war were of necessity kept to a minimum, and there are vast arrears to be made up. It has to be remembered that, owing to the cessation of new building, the average age of Great Western coaches to-day is 22 years, as compared with 18 years in 1939. The greater the age of the coach, of course, the greater the amount of repair work required to maintain it in a serviceable condition. Such is the vicious circle in which the technical departments are trying to force a breach.

A strong fleet of coaches is of great importance in maintaining not only the quantity of accommodation but its quality also. We have seen that where there are no coaches to spare in the shunting yard, more time is needed to make up trains, and trains are therefore delayed in starting. Too few coaches means bad timekeeping. Again, a shortage of coaches means that vehicles cannot be kept out of service long enough to do all that should be done in the matter of repairs and maintenance. Damaged upholstery cannot be renewed; empty lampholders remain empty; the cleaning of compartments has to be curtailed or postponed; less time is available for heating compartments before the coaches are formed into a train. Coaches, like human beings, must occasionally take time off from work if they are to be at their best, and they cannot take time off as long as the supply lags far behind the demand. It is largely for these reasons that the Great Western views the present shortage of coaches with the gravest anxiety. To increase the number of coaches in service is to-day a matter of the most pressing concern.

NEW METHODS AND MATERIALS

In new construction as well as in repair work, Great Western engineers are busy overhauling their methods to secure the highest possible output. Wherever possible, construction is being simplified with a view to economy in man-hours of labour. Commercial firms specialising in the application of new methods and materials have been called in to advise and assist. To increase the efficiency of the coach repair shop, the work is laid out on a continuous working line. New and specially designed equipment is constantly being added to speed up the processes. Several large flash butt welders have been installed: one for general repair work and another for three-link couplings. The time saved by these appliances is considerable. Metallurgical devices include new absorptiometer equipment for the rapid chemical analysis of metals and a spectroscopic apparatus for the immediate identification of alloy steels.

The traditional method of building a railway coach is, first, to build a complete body consisting of floor framing, side walls and roof, and afterwards to mount this body on the chassis or underframe. The new method now being applied on an increasing scale avoids the use of separate floor framing in the body ; the side pillars are secured direct to brackets welded to the underframe, which becomes the floor of the finished coach. It also introduces partial prefabrication on jig tables laid out in conjunction with the assembly line. On these tables are built twelve prefabricated frames which, when assembled, form the complete side and end walls of a coach. Minor changes in design will enable economies to be made in materials like timber, which are likely to remain in short supply for some time to come. The curvature of the side walls, for example, has been reduced for this reason.

Research is going on into the construction of light-weight coaches which should enable considerable economies in fuel to be made if they can be introduced on a substantial scale. In experimental coaches that have been built the weight is reduced by the use of light aluminium alloys and by highly efficient design. In some cases, the merits of several alternative materials are being tested in single coaches so that strictly comparative data may be obtained.

FREIGHT TRAINS

It was only to be expected that the conditions of freight train operation should have been even more severely affected by the war than those applying to passenger trains. The increase in the queues of wagons undergoing repair or out of service and waiting to be repaired is truly alarming: there were nearly 10,000 more wagons in these queues in 1946 than there were in 1938. The average age of a wagon before the war was the same as that of a passenger coach – eighteen years; it is twenty-one years to-day. The significance of this change is perhaps most forcibly brought home by the fact that the number of wagons between thirty and forty years old has gone up from 7,779 to 22,417, an increase of 188 per cent. This, as will be realised, is a difficult age-group.

Such changes as these are hardly calculated to induce complacency, and the Great Western is directing all its energies to the speeding up of new construction and repair work. Interesting results have already been achieved. The 1946-1947 building programme has as its object the placing into service of some 2,400 new vehicles of varying types, ranging from container flat wagons to forty-ton well trolleys. The majority of the new wagons will be specially equipped for use in express freight trains. A research department is busy studying the requirements of individual trades and industries and, in special circumstances, of individual firms. Where necessary, new types of wagons and other equipment are designed and built to meet these requirements. The development in recent years of door-to-door container transport is an interesting example. Despite the heavy burden carried during the war years, a progressive construction programme has been maintained, with the result that between 1939 and 1945 the stock of covered type containers for general purposes was increased by some 25 per cent. A further programme covering the next two years is in hand.

CONSTRUCTION VERSUS REPAIRS

The construction programme laid down for the Swindon works is determined not so much by the Railway's factory space and equipment for building coaches as by the supplies of materials and the number of workers that are available. For that reason, the Government is being continually pressed to allocate sufficient materials and labour for the full utilisation of the Railway's manufacturing and repairing capacity. Yet it is doubtful whether even in the most favourable circumstances the resources of the Swindon works would be sufficient to fill the gap created by unavoidable withdrawals.

Consider, first, the coach situation. The earliest and most optimistic programmes for 1946 called for the building of 260 new coaches, yet withdrawals for the same year were estimated to involve 322 vehicles in all. The deficit is being made up by bringing in the manufacturing facilities of independent firms of constructors.

With the consent of the Government, orders for seventy coaches were placed early in 1946. At the end of that year not one of these coaches had been delivered. Yet had they all been completed in time, the total net increase in the Company's fleet of coaches at the beginning of 1947 would still have been negligible. The material figure, however, is not the increase in the number of coaches owned but the increase in the number in actual service at any given moment. If the proportion of the fleet in daily service can be increased, the effect on train services will be the same as if a corresponding number of new coaches had been added.

And what of the freight side? There are to be some 2,400 new wagons of all types in the years 1946-47. Nevertheless, if withdrawals are taken into account, the year 1946 showed not a gain but an actual deficit, for the estimated number of wagons remaining at the end of the year was 87,923 as against 88,736 for the beginning, a net loss of more than 800. The rate of withdrawal will be high for all rolling stock during the next few years; there are special reasons why it must be especially heavy for freight wagons. One of these reasons is the difficulty of finding storage space for the 18,000 miscellaneous British railway wagons which are daily queueing up on Great Western tracks to await essential repairs. These wagons occupy seventy-four miles of running track and sidings which are urgently needed for the efficient working of goods services.

There are, then, two ways of adding to the number of vehicles in service: by new building or by accelerated repairs. Because the quickest results as well as the greatest output from the limited manpower are secured by the second method, the Great Western is concentrating the bulk of its resources on the repair of those vehicles which require a minimum of work to make them fit for service again. The policy is a short-term policy dictated by the need of the moment. Labour invested in a new rolling stock brings a better return in the long run than labour put into the repair of the old, but the short-term results of repair work are the greater, and at this moment quick results are essential. For vehicles needing more extensive repairs, the policy of scrapping is being intensified. A railway coach or wagon is not like a house, which can be made habitable by a few simple emergency repairs. The scrapping is costly to the Railway, but once again the public interest is put before all other considerations.

45

SPECIAL DUTY WAGONS

An interesting development in railway services before the war was the range of vehicles specially designed for the efficient handling of particular types of cargoes. One of these new vehicles is used not for a new class of cargo but for the oldest of all – coal. Since no less than 21 million tons of coal and coal type fuels were loaded at Great Western stations in 1945, it will be seen that the field for economy and efficiency is a large one. The traditional coal wagon may carry anything between ten and thirteen tons. The Great Western is a pioneer in the use of twenty-ton wagons on the heavy traffic routes to the industrial and export markets. The further development of the twenty-ton wagon is a special interest which the Railway will continue to pursue. Meanwhile, to encourage the use of higher capacity wagons generally, an all-steel wagon with a carrying capacity of sixteen tons has recently been designed to specifications agreed by all British railways, and the standardisation of such vehicles is now the subject of negotiations between the railways and those interested in the coal trade.

The shock-absorbing wagon is another type evolved for special uses. Some of the cargoes carried on the railways nowadays are not only highly perishable but so fragile that even the mildest shock may reduce their commercial value almost to vanishing point. Shunting operations as well as normal stopping and starting may involve considerable risk of jolting. Here is another challenge to the mechanical engineers. Their answer is a wagon in which the wagon body slides on the under-frame like a gun on its carriage. Heavy coil springs and rubber buffers are used to check its movement. The Great Western built some experimental shock-absorbing wagons shortly before the war, and at the beginning of 1947 it had altogether 106 such wagons in service. The wagons are used not only for articles of food like strawberries, peaches and eggs, but for fragile manufactured goods like glazed tiles and glassware. The question whether additional wagons are to be built depends on the volume of public demand.

For the conveyance of food, a traffic of special interest to the Great Western, the cooled refrigerator wagon is of crucial importance. The cooling agent used in these wagons may be either ordinary ice or the solid carbon-dioxide preparation known as dry ice. The quantity and the method of application are determined by the peculiarities of the traffic, the temperature at which it is required to be carried, the prevailing air temperature and the duration of the journey. The Great Western before the recent war owned a total of 636 refrigerator wagons for carrying meat and sausages (exclusive of 248 specially designed but not refrigerated). It is intended that this service shall be available for a wider range of goods, including fish, poultry, rabbits and soft fruit, and fifty additional wagons for use in passenger trains are on the immediate programme. Heated wagons are required as well as cooled ones. The Great Western banana services from Avonmouth to the big London distributing centres, for example, depend for their operation on six hundred banana wagons heated in the winter

EXPERIMENTAL FIRST-CLASS COMPARTMENT

1946

months to an even temperature of, roundly, 68 degrees Fahrenheit. Many of these wagons were used during the war for ordinary freight traffic, with the result that their equipment was damaged or put out of action by improper use; but the whole of the fleet was refitted for the 1946-7 winter traffic.

CONTAINERS AND TANKS

Of outstanding importance in the fast developing combined road-rail service is the fleet of containers which was built up over a period of years before the war. For the uninitiated it may be explained that a container is a detachable wagon body which is taken by lorry to or from the premises at which goods are to be loaded or unloaded. Great Western containers are designed for every type of commodity, from bulk merchandise, like bricks or grain, to finished articles such as bicycles or sanitary goods. Special types have been built for the safe conveyance of household removals, whilst for the traffic in perishable commodities there are insulated, ventilated and refrigerated containers. Immediately before the war the Great Western, after eighteen months of research and experiment, successfully evolved a large open container which carried cast-iron baths without packing. It need hardly be pointed out that these containers are now rendering an outstanding service in transporting one of the bulkiest components used in the Government's housing programme. Another type of container is the demountable road-rail tank for conveying different kinds of liquids without the use of casks or drums. (Tanks may also be built as permanent railway wagons, for traffic to and from premises having direct rail connections.) The Great Western is prepared to build tanks of various capacities to customers' own specifications and, where necessary, linings suitable for the different liquids carried are supplied with the tanks. Effective insulation can be incorporated; heating can be installed; and automatic discharge pumps can be fitted as a part of the vehicle body.

The advantages of containers and tanks are many: the handling of goods is reduced to a minimum; a door-to-door service is provided; materials and labour for packing are saved. In these days, with the prevailing shortages of raw material, this last point is becoming increasingly important. Considerable expansion is envisaged in the demand for containers, and the Great Western is not only building increased numbers of all types, but is also laying out specially designed yards at all the larger centres.

TRAINS OF THE FUTURE

Meanwhile, as work proceeds on the restoration of existing amenities, in the Railway's drawing offices and workshops the trains of the future are beginning to take shape. What will these trains be like?

To begin with, there will be more space in them. Space in a railway coach is rigidly restricted by the spacing and alignment of track and by the position and dimen-

WEYMOUTH STATION

PRELIMINARY DESIGN

sions of structures such as bridges, tunnels and station platforms. Within these limitations, the Great Western has always led the way in the development of larger and roomier coaches. The 70-foot coach, now superseded as unsuitable for the other railways, is remembered by many as an outstanding conception in modern rolling stock design. The new standard Great Western coach (64 feet long over ends, 63 feet over corners) is at the moment of writing the longest standard passenger railway coach in the British Isles. Consideration is being given to the standardisation of such a coach for British railways generally. Since coaches before the war were designed to lengths varying between 55 feet and 61 feet, it will be seen that there is considerable increase in the space available for compartments as well as for toilets.

NEW INTERIORS

The interiors of the new trains will be very different from the old. Already some of the coaches with new fittings and furnishings have gone into operation, and the travelling public has shown unmistakable signs that the changes are generally welcomed and approved.

Perhaps the most striking of these changes is the use of fluorescent lighting. The advantages of this form of lighting were discovered during the war by many thousands of workers in factories and offices concerned with important war contracts. Its development since the war has been rapid. On a railway journey a plentiful supply of light of a pleasing and restful colour is particularly important because of the increase in the habit of reading. One difficult problem in the lighting of a railway compartment is to strike the right balance between general lighting (which must be at high level so that the contents of luggage racks can be seen) and individual lighting for the benefit of the seated passenger. In its new first-class compartments, the Great Western has taken the bold step of concentrating an unusually high proportion of the total lighting in the individual reading lights. These lights are concealed in the fronts of the luggage racks so that there is complete freedom from dazzle. The lighting in these compartments is such an advance on pre-war practice that it is difficult to speak of it except in superlatives. It may be best, therefore, to refrain from further comment and leave the reader to discover it for himself.

Next after lighting, the most interesting development in coach interiors is the use of plastics for wall and partition linings and for fittings generally. The cleanliness of a plastic surface is comparable to that of a glazed faience tile. More attention than ever is now being paid to the easy and efficient cleaning of trains and to the maintenance of a clean appearance at all times, and plastic materials have proved especially useful in this respect. Lining and covering materials for floors, walls, partitions, ceilings and all furnishings are being selected as a result of exhaustive tests of their properties of dirt resistance and cleanability. The greatest and most uncompromising use of plastics will, of course, be found in the more utilitarian portions of the train – in corridors, sleeping compartments and lavatories, where traditional ideas of interior decoration play a smaller part than they do elsewhere.

The refitted restaurant cars have become widely familiar to travellers on the Great Western since the first of them took its opening run on 31 December, 1945. The first-class saloon (see the illustration on page 13) has wall linings veneered in blistered sapeli with contrasting bandings; the curtains are bronze-coloured cotton damask with a small beige design; the chairs are covered with smoke-blue leather edged with beige pipings. Light fittings of pink flashed opal glass are recessed into the ceiling. The wall linings in the third-class saloon are a combination of mottled ash with heavily-marked zebrano: the seat uph olstery is a light tan colour, and the floor covering beige and green. A notable feature in both saloons is the softness and warmth of colour in the artificial lighting.

In the sleeping cars, too, extensive use is being made of decorative leather coverings. Quilted leather is being used, for example, on the head and foot panels of the beds. Various types of lining a re being tried for the walls – mainly plastic sheeting and panels of plastic impregnated fabrics, though new types of veneer are also used. Lighting, heating and ventilation are improved; thermos bottles will keep drinking water cool for travellers who like a well-warmed place to sleep in. While the structure remains the same, these very thorough renovations have produced a sleeping compartment very different in comfort and appearance from that of the nineteen-thirties.

DESIGN RESEARCH

In planning these and other new amenities for the railway traveller, the Railway's experts are drawing upon their long experience of the public's needs and preferences. The lessons taught by more than a century of railway operation form a body of experience that is a valuable guide in the solution of many problems of design. There is no substitute for the direct, hard-won experience gathered by successive generations.

The Great Western, however, is a forward-looking railway. It holds the view that the first need in a great public service like transport is that there shall exist among the management a perfect understanding of the requirements of those who use it. It also knows that past experience, however valuable it may be, can never supply the whole of the answer. The conditions of railway traffic never stand still; what is good to-day may be hopelessly inadequate to-morrow. The scientific study of changing conditions is the foundation of successful railway management. For example, to ascertain the extent of the demand for train services between different points and at different times, Great Western experts carefully analyse the many letters and telephone enquiries which reach the management in the course of a year. The trend of traffic is plotted by means of information obtained at regular intervals through local passenger counts. At holiday times, careful forecasts are made of the probable volume of traffic so that a suitable number of additional trains may be kept ready for service at a few minutes' notice. Before the war, the number of advance seat reservations furnished a useful index for the purpose of these calculations; this index is not generally available to-day, and other sources of information have to be drawn upon.

In the Railway's research departments and drawing offices the same precise, scientific methods are being applied to physical requirements in passenger accommodation. First in order of importance is the full utilisation of the available space for the arrangement of reclining bodies and extended limbs as well as for the movement of passengers from one part of the train to another. These are the big fundamental problems of planning and circulation. The value of all subsequent efforts may depend on these problems being correctly solved. They include the design and equipment of toilets and all those amenities that make the whole difference between the freedom and ease of railway travel and the strain and discomfort of many other forms of locomotion.

The structure having been determined in its main outline, there come a number of highly technical questions as, for example, the heating, thermal insulation, ventilation, lighting and sound-proofing of carriages and compartments. How warm should a compartment be? At which point should the heat be applied so as to give the greatest sense of comfort to all the occupants alike? How quickly do passengers expect a compartment to regain its warmth when heat has been lost through the opening of doors or other causes? What capacity for heat input does this rate of recovery require? What is the amount of heat transmittance that can be permitted in a floor if cold feet are to be avoided, or in a wall if it is not to give passengers the feeling that it is "radiating" cold? What is the maximum relative humidity that is compatible with a sense of comfort and well-being at different seasons of the year? How much air must be introduced per minute or per hour to give passengers a sensation of comfortable freshness? How much to avoid condensation in restaurant cars and other places where the air is liable to contain a high degree of moisture? How and where should this air be introduced to avoid draughts? These and many other questions are no longer left to be dealt with under the rule-of-thumb practices of the past. There is a correct scientific answer for each of them, and the Great Western is taking steps to discover that answer and to make it the foundation of its specifications and designs.

Again, there is the subtle and intricate problem of the design of seating. Passengers vary considerably in height, in breadth, in weight, in length of limb and in many other characteristics. They also vary in their ideas of what constitutes a comfortable seated posture. These and many other factors will influence the height, depth and width of seats, the question whether or not a seat should be truly horizontal, the length, shape and inclination of the back, the softness or hardness of the upholstery, the height and shape of the arm rests, and other details of design. There is the problem of deciding the most suitable size and shape for doors and windows, the most convenient gear for opening and closing, the ideal position and design for light fittings for general and localised lighting, the most useful shape for luggage racks and the correct placing of hand rails and handles. In all such matters, the technique of the modern investigator will help to make the trains of the future worthy of this democratic age.

The scientific approach to a full understanding of human requirements is not an easy one. The investigator will be concerned with a few big questions and with a multitude of little ones any of which may prove of decisive importance. More and more, modern science tends to attach value to minutiæ, to the little things that matter. When doctors, for example, study the nutritive qualities of bread, it is not to the main constituents such as protein and carbo-hydrate that they give first attention, but to the microscopic quantities of amino-acids, minerals and vitamins that play such a big part in maintaining health. In the provision of a healthy and comfortable environment, the correct solution is often built up from the sum of many little answers. The plans of all the departments of the Great Western, and not least of that department whose functions include the design and construction of coaches, are founded on the broad principle that where the interests of the public are concerned no detail is too trivial to turn the second best into the best – the best that was so well described by a well-known living critic[1] when he spoke of "paradises on wheels, clean, fast, silent, superbly windowed, wonderfully catered for."

[1]Editorial article in *Horizon*, February, 1946.

CHAPTER FIVE · THE MEN

TEAM WORK

THE MEN and women of the Great Western have always shown an exceptional capacity for working together as a united team. Experience has taught them the importance of solidarity, which is something more than mere co-operation. They know how it can not only magnify the individual's contribution to the common job but also increase his own private happiness and satisfaction. To-day, they have behind them nearly a century and a quarter of corporate existence, strengthened by a continuity of leadership and a consistency of policy unusual among public or commercial undertakings. The men at all levels are united by the confidence and the understanding that only a long and intimate partnership can beget. Speaking in Birmingham in March, 1946, the Prime Minister, Mr. Attlee, expressed his conviction that "the most efficient industries in this country are those wherein there is mutual trust between the employers and employed." Measured by such a standard, the Railway is paramount among efficient industries.

One small example of this remarkable group feeling may be taken at random from many thousands. In September, 1945, a few days after the details of the Great Western experiments with oil burning locomotives were first made known, there was delivered in the General Manager's office a long letter from an old railwayman who had served with the Railway as a locomotive fireman at the beginning of this century. For private reasons he had resigned his position in 1903 to go abroad. While working as a locomotive foreman and inspector in South America he had gained considerable experience in the handling of oil burning locomotives. And so this one-time fireman, now retired, after an absence of forty-two years had taken up his pen to wish his old firm success in this venture, and to give a mass of detailed technical advice, the fruit of years of personal experience in foreign countries. Loyalty and affection of this high order are usually associated with regiments and schools. They are strong among the people of this Railway. In them is to be found the secret of team work in the Great Western sense.

Good conditions of employment do not of themselves produce perfect teamwork, but no teamwork of any kind is possible without them. Much praise has been given to

54

the conditions under which the railwayman works in this country. National wage rates and conditions of service are agreed between the managements and the trade unions. On the rare occasions when difficulty is found in reaching agreement, the matter is referred to a national wages tribunal, an independent body set up by the railways in 1935. The machinery, which works so well that the Railway has not known a single major disturbance for twenty years, has been described as the most highly developed industrial conciliation machinery to be found in this or any other country. Yet no one will ever regard it as final and perfect; ways and means of securing even closer and fuller co-operation are constantly being pursued. No wonder an important newspaper was able recently to state that there is no better atmosphere to be found in any industry in this country than that which exists on the railways.

RECRUITMENT AND EDUCATION

The men of the Great Western are an asset built up and strengthened over long periods of time. The effectiveness of this asset has been seriously impaired by the war. The 14,483 men who joined the forces were replaced by women and by recruits of inferior attainments and physique. The old tradition of teamwork and devotion to a common purpose was strong enough even for these shocks, but the loss in skill and experience cannot be computed. At the end of the war, the men of sixty-five and upwards remaining in active employment numbered well over three thousand. Demobilisation was slow; the bulk of it fell under the normal group release scheme; notwithstanding the vital importance of railway transport, releases under Class B were granted for 719 men only. Twelve months after V.J. Day, more than six thousand Great Western workers were still serving with the armed forces, waiting to return.

To build up the post-war personnel, recruits are being sought for all departments. At the end of 1946, over 5,700 essential posts were waiting to be filled. Since the work is responsible and the standards high, recruitment cannot proceed very quickly. A good type of man is needed, having a high standard of intelligence and physical fitness, and capable of developing that delight and pride in his work which is the secret of the Great Western service.

For many years, close study has been given to the problem of providing wider opportunities for the staff through schemes for special education and training. Boys and girls recruited for the clerical staff at school-leaving age are encouraged to attend evening classes organised by local education authorities for English, shorthand, mathematics and other subjects. As they progress in their work and in their studies, opportunities are afforded to them (and also to staff recruited at later ages) to attend University and other courses in railway subjects, such as those of the London School of Economics. The cost of this training is borne by the Railway. For the instruction of staff in shorthand and typewriting, day classes have been organised and are conducted by members of the staff. Studentships at technical colleges are awarded to promising technical apprentices in the department of the Chief Mechanical Engineer. Courses of instruction in signalling and the safe working of railways held under the Company's own auspices at various centres are open to all members of the staff. The lecturers are expert members of the Railway's organisation. The lecture rooms at Paddington and certain other centres are equipped for demonstration purposes with a miniature section of railway complete with signalling apparatus, and actual signal-box appliances are also used. Similar classes open to all grades are held in station accountancy, station working, and railway salesmanship.

There are courses specifically designed for manual workers in which practical and theoretical instruction is combined according to the nature of the work. For example, courses of instruction are held at various centres to enable permanent-way men to extend their knowledge of the theory and practice of permanent-way maintenance and kindred operations, and schools have been established at Bristol and Birmingham for the training of staff in signal and telegraph installation and maintenance work.

The work of education is further pursued and developed by the men themselves by means of lecture and debating societies which are given all encouragement and assistance by the Railway. Most of the societies, like the London Lecture and Debating Society, run lending libraries for members, and their ancillary activities include the award of essay prizes which are keenly competed for.

PRACTICAL TRAINING

To reap the full benefit of educational programmes such as these, the teaching courses are supplemented by practical training under normal conditions of working. The system of training is a flexible one and is constantly expanding to meet new conditions and new needs. The following example, chosen at random, will indicate the comprehensive nature of these schemes and the wide range of opportunities to which they provide the key.

Staff who have obtained a Certificate of Merit in, say, the signalling or station accounts examinations (or a corresponding certificate awarded in connection with a recognised external course) are eligible for consideration for a course of training which normally takes three years to complete. During the period of training candidates are paid a salary rising by annual increments. An elaborate timetable is laid down so that a wide field of experience may be covered in the allotted time. For example, a trainee selected from the traffic department will start with three months' work at a small station and three at a larger one, followed by another three months in a marshalling yard. After some experience in the departments responsible for locomotive running and signals, he has longer spells in the office of a Divisional Superintendent and in the headquarters office of the Superintendent of the Line (the manager in charge of operation).

A final three months as a station master completes the course. Progress reports are prepared at regular intervals by the trainee himself and by the officers in charge of his studies. Courses planned on very much the same lines are available for a limited number of new staff entering the service from the Universities. University trainees are nominated by official sponsors such as the University Appointments Boards.

The effectiveness of these courses of training has been clearly proved. To-day, among the successful trainees who have risen from humble beginnings are some of the most highly valued and respected members of the Railway's staff, including a number of Assistant Divisional Superintendents and Assistant District Goods Managers, and several in still higher ranks.

On the engineering side, trainees known as Civil Engineering Cadets are given special opportunities of acquiring knowledge of practical civil engineering in its various branches, including constructional works, bridges, permanent way, structural steelwork, and general engineering on railways and docks. There are two courses for Cadets – the three-year graduate course and the five-year course for non-graduates (graduate Cadets must first have obtained a degree recognised by the Institution of Civil Engineers as equivalent to Sections A and B of the Associate Membership Examination of the Institution). A similar Cadet course is available in signal and telegraph engineering.

THE EX-SERVICE MAN

The training schemes generally are designed in the first place for the younger men showing exceptional promise and ability. Their purpose is to enlarge the knowledge and experience of such men in the various branches of their departments. During the immediate post-war period, however, having regard to the exceptional conditions brought about by the war, the older men also are given an opportunity of enrolling. There are staff returning from the Forces who in their war service have shown themselves possessed of qualities that should fit them for positions of greater responsibility; similar qualities may also be shown by men who have remained with the Railway during the war period. A training scheme has been established which will give these men an opportunity of qualifying for vacancies in higher positions that may occur during the next few years; (selection for training, however, does not carry with it any promise of special promotion). Candidates for this special training also include University graduates and those who have passed through the Business Training Scheme recently instituted by the Ministry of Labour. Training courses are being individually planned to suit the age, experience and other qualifications of each candidate. A special allowance over and above the basic salary is granted for the period of training; and lodging and out-of-pocket expenses are allowed as necessary.

It is many years now since the Great Western first became known as a pioneer in staff education. That reputation was earned not only by the volume of educational activity but still more by its qualities of variety and breadth of scope. The governing purpose in these schemes has always been to develop the maximum of expert skill while avoiding the narrowing and inhibiting influences of specialisation. A large organisation like the Great Western with its staff of 119,000 cannot be fully efficient without a strictly departmentalised pattern in which every worker knows his allotted place. But departmentalisation should be flexible and dynamic; it should be a servant and not a master. Through all the adaptations and modifications necessitated by the changing conditions of these times, staff education and training with this Railway will mean the development of key men who can lift their eyes above the daily task to survey the full picture, and who can impart a sense of that wider meaning to fellow workers in all ranks.

HOUSING AND LODGING

The housing of railway workers presents few special problems when houses are in good supply at all points of the system. Conditions of shortage, however, are apt to hit the railway worker particularly hard. Promotion in his job will often involve a transfer to another locality. Traffic requirements and other extraneous circumstances may affect him in the same way. So that it might assist in meeting the housing needs of its workers, the Railway in 1923 obtained Parliamentary powers which enabled it to co-operate with the men in the formation of Housing Societies. Before the recent war, a total of 1,646 houses had been built by Great Western Housing Societies in places as far apart as London and Penzance, involving an expenditure of nearly one million pounds. These houses, which were laid out in independent estates each with its elected local Committee of Management composed of tenant employees, made it possible for many railwaymen with their families to live in pleasant and healthy surroundings within reasonable distance of their place of work.

In August, 1944, in anticipation of the present difficulties, the Railway announced that it was prepared to consider the extension of existing housing estates and the formation of additional Housing Societies in new centres. Under the Housing (Financial and Miscellaneous Provisions) Act, 1946, which provides for the payment of subsidies, schemes were put forward which, with the financial assistance contemplated by the Act, should allow of houses being provided to let at a rental which the workers can reasonably be expected to pay. As there is no profit motive in the Great Western scheme, which aims at providing houses for letting only under the management of the staff themselves, no difficulty should arise in securing the necessary consents. Negotiations with the Councils of Didcot, Swansea, Banbury, Ealing and Hayes are still proceeding at the moment of writing, and an attempt will be made to carry out schemes at other centres on the Great Western system where railwaymen are urgently in need of housing. So long as there are Great Western workers who are unable to find proper accommodation this important activity will go on.

In addition to building family dwellings, the Railway is providing hostel accommodation for railwaymen in various parts of its system. There are two kinds of hostels, those for travelling workers, mostly train crews, men with a home of their own whose duties require them to spend occasional nights away – and those for men transferred to certain centres who have been unable to get lodging or housing accommodation.

The former type of worker presents a special problem. The necessity for lodging away from home is one which the management is desirous of keeping within the smallest practicable dimensions. During the war period steps were taken to reduce the number of turns of duty involving lodging away from home. These arrangements have, however, resulted in a loss of efficiency in the train service. Engine crews have had to be changed more frequently on the way; every such change is a potential cause of delay. If the train services are to be restored to their high pre-war standard of efficiency and punctuality, it is inevitable that the changes of crews should be reduced. This means more "lodging turns." But private lodgings are not as easy to obtain as they were; they are particularly difficult for workers whose duties require them to keep somewhat unusual hours. Those that are available do not always prove satisfactory. The Great Western, having made a detailed study of these difficulties, has decided to give an important place in its post-war programme to the provision of clean and attractive quarters where "double home" men may sleep in comfort and enjoy their leisure hours.

Other amenities which will play a part in ensuring the well-being of railwaymen are canteens, messrooms, locker rooms, and drying rooms. Better lavatories and bicycle sheds are a regular part of the programmes. For all these amenities new standards have been laid down so that the improvements made possible by post-war building technique may not be lacking.

RAILWAYMEN AT PLAY

After the day's work come the social, cultural and recreational activities that have always been highly developed among the Great Western folk. The events organised by the Staff Association in and around its thirty-four Institutes (the figure is that for 1939) are famous in the West Country and their fame has travelled elsewhere. For number, variety and popularity there can be few to equal them. These people have shown that they understand the art of social living in the widest sense of the term.

Here, by way of illustration, are some of the things with which the Great Western men and women occupied their leisure hours in the year 1938, when peace was still peace. A three-day Annual Conference attended by delegates from all parts of the Great Western system. A Music and Drama Festival lasting five days during which twenty-one separate sessions were held to adjudicate on the performance of over two thousand competitors in eighty-four classes. At this Festival, thirty-two awards were made for vocal and instrumental music (including chamber music, orchestras and military bands), drama, literature and public speaking. An arts and crafts competition with awards for painting, drawing and various crafts including model making. Swimming races, matches in every indoor and outdoor game; a horticultural show; a fur and feather show. Lectures, demonstrations, organised visits to factories, excursions, parties for grown-ups, parties for children. The list could be extended for quite another page.

Roundly one in three of all Great Western workers are active participants in Staff Association affairs. The men have expressed their desire to resume these spare-time interests at the earliest possible moment, and the Railway for its part is anxious to help. Unfortunately, some of the bigger events involve a considerable amount of travel. Accommodation on trains is short, and the general public has first claim on that which is available. A beginning, however, was made in 1946 with local events involving a minimum of transport; the resumption of the Festival had to be postponed till March, 1947, when it is likely to show a record in the number of musical and other classes.

The team spirit of the Great Western shows itself in many ways. The traveller finds that he is served with something more than efficiency. He notices the men's genuine interest in his well-being while in their care. He marvels at the obvious pride and affection with which they enter into their daily labours. But behind these surface manifestations lies a field of social collaboration of which he is little aware. It is the strength and depth of this wider teamwork, which extends far beyond the hours of work on the railway, that form the scattered workers of the Railway into an organism that is living indeed.

CHAPTER SIX · STATIONS

SPRING CLEAN

THE end of the war saw the beginning of the biggest spring-cleaning job in the Great Western's history. Six years of reduced maintenance had left their mark on station and other buildings. Deterioration was visibly setting in and it was necessary that its progress should be stopped without delay. The 1946 repainting programme alone is estimated to have cost £140,000 for one hundred stations of varying sizes, from Paddington downwards.

The engineers responsible for making up these arrears of maintenance are working under an onerous handicap. They have at the same time to undertake the removal of the many defence installations on which so much time and money was expended from 1938 onwards. For another fifteen months, manpower which is urgently needed for maintenance work must be diverted to this business of dismantling and demolishing the paraphernalia of war. Until at least the end of 1947 the double task will put a heavy strain on the Railway's resources in labour as well as in tools and plant.

There is also war damage to be repaired. The amount of work required is considerable. Take, for example, the replacement of glass in roofs: 120,000 square feet for Paddington, 115,000 for the transit sheds at Swansea Docks, 100,000 for Birmingham (Snow Hill), 80,000 for Tyseley locomotive shed – only a little short of ten acres of glass at these four places alone. The structure of roofs has suffered, too. Temporary coverings of roofing felt and asbestos cement sheeting did not protect roof timbers or glazing bars from exposure to moisture; a single station like Bristol (Temple Meads) may require a thousand cubic feet of timber for essential repairs. And so it goes on throughout the system.

Here and there this great spring clean is already causing remarkable changes in the streets of our cities. Railway stations that a short while ago seemed (if possible) even more dismally begrimed than the streets around them are beginning to assume an aspect of gaiety and good cheer. In many cases, the architecture of these stations reveals new charms, charms that one hardly suspected in the days before the war. There was, for example, the roof of Paddington. We knew that this roof had been acclaimed by experts as one of the most interesting examples of nineteenth century architecture in iron to be seen in any country. Yet how many travellers six years ago were able to appreciate its beauties? When in early spring of 1946, the black-out was lifted, the sunlight that fell again on those slight and elegant traceries was caught by the bloom of new buff-coloured paint. The effect was rather like the cleaning of an old master; the well-remembered pattern was unchanged, but the features appeared with the freshness of a revelation.

PLANS AND PRIORITIES

It seems likely that the next twenty-five years in this country will be a period of unexampled physical reconstruction. The railways are fortunate in entering upon this period with many hundreds of stations that for one reason or another have become obsolescent and therefore ripe for scrapping. The Great Western is conscious that this opportunity for enterprising modernisation is a priceless one which may not occur again for some considerable time. Its plans are being formed accordingly. The experts know that they will be building not for the needs of this year or next year, but for the needs of the next generation. They are determined in their building to get a running start of the obsolescence that comes inevitably to the works of man. In doing this they are willing to run the risk of occasionally building a little ahead of their time.

It was some years before the war that the Railway's engineers and architects first began to study the fresh problems to be solved and to sketch out tentative solutions. Many of these schemes – mainly the more ambitious ones – will necessarily be held up until labour and materials become more freely available. A short priority list has, however, been prepared with which it is hoped to make substantial progress during the next five years.

At the head of this list comes the completion of certain schemes planned in connection with the facilities afforded by the Railways (Agreement) Act of 1935. But many other stations besides those included in the 1935 schemes are now in the list. The list is a long one, with Paddington looming large towards the latter end. Unfortunately the chances of this list being translated into a dated programme are at the moment somewhat remote. Of course there is nothing the Great Western would like better than to work to a timetable. In normal times, it would of course have dealt with these stations in their order of urgency, a subject upon which the Railway has very clear and definite ideas. Now, much will depend on the time required for securing the necessary approval and agreement from local authorities and the many other interests concerned. The speed at which supplies of labour, materials and component parts can be made available is another controlling factor. Moreover, the technical departments have not only to prepare plans and designs for the new schemes, they must also review and where necessary revise the whole of the plans drawn up before the war, having regard both to changing conditions of traffic and to the new post-war level of costs. This task has placed a heavy burden on the existing organisation.

It will be seen that however pressing the need may be, and whatever may be the desire of the Railway or its passengers, the sequence of these works will depend on what becomes possible from one week to the next. The first stations to be rebuilt will inevitably be those where the preparatory work meets with the fewest delays and obstructions.

STANDARDS OF DESIGN

And what of the appearance of the new stations? How and where will they reflect the demands of the pots-war traveller, those new demands coloured and stimulated by the development of motor cars, of long-distance coaches, of holiday camps, of liners and ocean cruises and passenger aircraft and all the rest? What is the Great Western doing to create that new environment in which the speed, comfort and cleanliness of modern railway travel will come into its own and find full and clear expression?

The Great Western lives by selling travel. Travel takes place in trains. It was natural, therefore, that the Railway for many years past should have given trains its first consideration. It has been said that Great Western trains are the best groomed trains in the world. However that may be, it was abundantly clear before the war that in the design, the painting, the furnishing and the equipment of these trains only the best was thought good enough, and that no trouble was spared in day-to-day cleaning and maintenance work to maintain the high standard of appearance set by the constructors. To-day, the Great Western recognises as a first principle the necessity for making its stations worthy of its trains.

The station, indeed, is the introduction or prologue to the train; its relation to the train is that of the first course in an attractive and well-chosen meal. The relation may also be described as that of the frame to the picture; and many a picture has been spoilt by indifferent framing. Again, there is also the junction station which comes as an interlude between the two train journeys. Such a station is Swindon. The Railway is giving considerable thought to Swindon. Having spent more than a century making train journeys more and more pleasant and restful, it now intends to make sure that the approach to those journeys reaches a similar high standard of comfort and amenity.

Occasional references to the new standards laid down for station design will be found at different points in this account. The new standards may be summarised here for convenience.

    a. Free and comfortable circulation planned as a result of a scientific study of passenger movement; circulation unencumbered by luggage trolleys for which separate means of access will be planned.

    b. The various station and platform buildings grouped into compact and continuous blocks.

c. Clearly distinguishable signs, illuminated where necessary, to guide and inform passengers at all points between their entering and leaving.

d. Escalators to and from different levels, wherever the traffic is sufficient to justify their operation.

e. Island platforms to allow direct interchange from one train to another, without climbing stairs.

f. Full-length platforms to avoid double stopping, protected from the weather for most of their length, and fitted with windscreens to protect passengers from cold winds and draughts.

g. Plentiful lighting in hours of darkness in all parts where passengers may tread.

h. At the very large stations, interesting and well-stocked shops in which last-minute shopping will become a pleasant experience.

i. Shops, kiosks, automatic machines and advertisements arranged in compliance with a general station design and rigorously controlled so that order and dignity may never be lacking.

j. Light, airy waiting rooms, well heated, well ventilated, welcoming in appearance, decorated in light, cheerful colours.

k. Tea and coffee served in the waiting room, or in refreshment rooms next door.

l. Bright, welcoming refreshment rooms and restaurants, with soft, intimate lighting, scrupulously clean underfoot, without advertisements, lined where necessary with absorbent materials that will reduce noise and clatter.

m. The windows of waiting rooms, refreshment rooms, buffets and restaurants arranged so as to give a full view of platforms and trains.

n. Lavatories lined with delicately coloured tiles and kept spotlessly clean at all hours of the day and night.

An indication of the new standard of design applying to waiting rooms is given in the illustration which appears as a frontispiece to this book.

FOOD AND DRINK

There are on the stations of the Great Western system 138 restaurants, licensed refreshment rooms, and tea rooms, with three quick-lunch snack bars. In 1939 meals served averaged 1,670 a day; cups of tea 18,000 a day.

It will be some time before the lifting of food restrictions enables the Railway's catering to be restored to its pre-war quality, variety and volume. It will be still longer before the number of places serving meals and refreshments can be increased. But as and when new stations are built or old stations overhauled or reconstructed, important improvements will be made to all these premises.

The standards that have been laid down will bring light and gaiety as well as greater efficiency in service. The planning will be radically different. Windows will be opened up to give broad views of the platforms and the trains. This will necessarily entail some loss of privacy; but privacy is not nowadays appreciated as it used to be. The line of demarcation between waiting rooms and tea-rooms will tend to be less sharply defined; in many new waiting rooms passengers will drink tea or coffee while they wait.

The inside appearance of the new rooms will also change. Fewer dark coloured materials will be used; timbers generally will be light in colour, and dark grey marble counter tops will seldom be seen. The scale of the interiors will be more companionable; ceilings will be lowered to a more suitable height and the counters and other furnishings will shed some of their traditional bulk. Instead of advertisements there will be pleasant pictures on the walls. The lighting will be more intimate and at the same time more efficient.

NEW STATIONS

It has been said that the choice of Great Western stations to be rebuilt during the next few years will be largely determined by factors beyond the Railway's control. The following particulars, therefore, are given mainly as an illustration of the range and variety of the work to be done.

On every section of the line, stations are to be found where the traffic has completely outgrown the original buildings just as the trains have outgrown the platforms which were first constructed with plenty of length to spare. When a platform is too short to accommodate a full-length train of twelve coaches, the train has to pull up twice to allow passengers to alight from and to board all parts of the train. Now, double stopping is a makeshift which both the Railway and its passengers cordially dislike. It is one of the greatest enemies of good timekeeping. The Great Western, therefore, started some time before the recent war to lengthen the platforms at a number of stations. The works authorised under the Railways (Agreement) Act, 1935, included the lengthening of platforms at many stations including those on the branch lines to Barnstaple in Devonshire and to Minehead in Somerset, which were completed before the war. Newquay station, another of these, is to be entirely rebuilt, with an interesting new development in the form of an outside luggage-in-advance section capable of dealing promptly with the luggage of summer holiday travellers even when the volume reaches its highest peak.

Other stations to be rebuilt are Weymouth (see the illustration on page 49), where a large tea room which is under consideration would provide an attractive new social centre; Swindon, whose new hotel is referred to in another chapter, and Westbury, where a new central signal box will help to control train movements more efficiently and economically than is possible with the two existing boxes. At all these stations the platforms are to be extended to the full standard length.

NEXT STATION

THE QUESTION OF TRACKS

There are, however, other cases where the obsolescence of a station arises from the capacity and layout of the track accommodation rather than from the state of the building. For example, at Snow Hill station, Birmingham, the number of main line tracks is to be increased, possibly by transforming two existing bays into through tracks. This important improvement scheme has enabled the Railway to give serious consideration to a plan which projects the main concourse westwards over the tracks, with escalators to and from the platforms below. The escalator installation, if it is proceeded with, would probably be the first on the Great Western system and might well be the first on any main line station in this country (excepting those communicating with Underground stations, of which several were in existence before the war). The use and operation of such escalators would undoubtedly be studied so that other installations may benefit from the experience thus gathered.

Reading is one of the busiest junction stations on the Great Western. The main line from Paddington divides here into its two principal routes. The traffic from the south and south-east coast flows in via Newbury, Basingstoke and Guildford. To relieve the pressure on the four main tracks – two up and two down – an additional track was laid down in the eighteen-nineties to provide for the passage of the many up trains that run through the station daily without stopping. The addition of this track released valuable platform space for stopping trains, with the result that delays were reduced, and improvements could be made in the train services, more particularly on Saturdays, when the line is busiest. Similar benefits might have been expected from a through track for down trains, but the physical difficulties were more serious in proportion, and the work was deferred. This second through track stands high on the Great Western priority list, and when Reading station becomes due for general reconstruction the work will almost certainly be put in hand as part of the larger scheme. Services to Plymouth, Fishguard, Oxford and many other places should benefit considerably.

For the new station at Bath, again, one of the proposals under consideration would provide through tracks serving two full-length island platforms. A roughly similar arrangement is contemplated for the new station at Weston-super-Mare; in fact, more and more the pair of island platforms serving four tracks will tend to become the accepted pattern for medium size stations of this type.

At Exeter (St. David's), it is possible that Southern Railway services may have their own tracks and island platforms allotted to them on the west side of the station; additional lines from St. David's to Cowley Bridge would enable Southern trains to and from Central station to circulate independently of Great Western trains. Three full-length platforms would be available for Great Western trains only. The goods services will be transferred to a new site at the north end of the station, where a new goods depot, warehouse and loading dock will be built, with new cattle pens and marshalling yards. A scheme for a new bridge across the railway and the river Exe, which would link the city with Exwick, is under consideration.

JOINT STATIONS

Changing circumstances since 1939 have brought new opportunities as well as new problems. Schemes which were drawn up on simplified lines have been given deeper and more comprehensive study; interests other than those immediately concerned have been consulted and have given, or appear likely to give, their agreement or support. Outstanding examples of such schemes are the new stations for Oxford and Banbury. In each case, there is a clear possibility that plans which, as originally authorised, were concerned with the rebuilding of the Great Western stations only, may now be expanded to include the amalgamation of adjacent Great Western and L.M.S. stations into larger single stations of the most modern design.

At Oxford, there is now a station with two single-sided platforms for main line trains and two bays for local services to and from Banbury, Worcester and other places. On the east side of the station is a small terminal station belonging to the L.M.S. Trains from this station serve local stations north of Oxford and also connect with main line trains to the north. Clearly the ideal solution would be for the site to be developed by the Great Western and the L.M.S., in consultation with the Oxford City Council, to give improved approaches including a bus station and car park.

The new combined station might appropriately lie closer to the main Botley Road approach and just east of the existing Great Western station. The present station building, which has now become obsolete, is built at the level of the platforms and is reached from the Botley Road below by an inclined roadway sloping up from the main road. Passengers intending to travel down the line have now to go down again from the high level station into a subway leading to the down platform. If the new station could be built at the lower (subway) level, circulation would be considerably freer and more convenient. The passenger subway could be a long hall twenty to thirty feet wide; in accordance with the new Great Western standards for station planning, the movement of passengers would be completely separated from that of luggage trucks. It would be possible to provide new and improved goods sheds and yards at the London end of the station, and substantial extensions to the locomotive depot at the Banbury end.

The existing Great Western station at Banbury is a modest structure with a single-sided platform on each side of a double track. Communication between the two is by way of a footbridge. There is a bay for L.N.E.R. trains to the north. The small L.M.S. terminal station which adjoins provides for local services to Bletchley and Towcester.

The station building is at platform level; the approach road turns out of Bridge Street by the side of the Oxford Canal. In this case it would be preferable for a new combined station to be placed at high level, at the point where Bridge Street runs over the railway. Passengers would walk straight from Bridge Street into a large, well-lighted main concourse. From this public concourse they would pass into a smaller train concourse with staircases and luggage lifts. Below, two new island platforms would be served by four main line tracks. L.N.E.R. trains could use a bay platform at the northern end and L.M.S. trains another on the London side. There would be room for a car park for a hundred cars adjoining the station.

An important part of the Banbury proposals is the re-alignment of the curve on which the station stands. With the curve as now constructed, no train may pass through the station at more than sixty miles an hour. This restriction is particularly onerous because the station lies in a depression with a rising gradient on either side of it. The new tracks will make it possible for the maximum speed to be raised to seventy-five miles an hour. That express services to Birmingham and beyond will benefit goes without saying.

ROAD IMPROVEMENTS

With the increased size and scope of these schemes, it has become necessary that they should be carefully fitted into larger developments sponsored by local town and country planning authorities. Hence, before the Great Western can finalise its own plans, there must be decisions on many vital matters including, for example, road traffic requirements and building heights. The stations for Oxford and Banbury rank high in the list of priorities; but in their new and improved form it will take time to develop them fully. Only one thing could have reconciled the Railway to the idea of further delay, and that is a firm conviction that the stations when completed will more than justify its perseverance.

In some cases, improvements to Great Western tracks and platforms will be carried out in conjunction with important road and bridge works planned by local authorities. Combined operations of this kind provide exceptional opportunities for dealing with station approaches as well as with the stations themselves. Perhaps the most interesting examples of such reconstruction schemes are those associated with the two Devonshire stations of Paignton and Goodrington; projected improvements include new bridges over the railway which are to take the place of existing level crossings.

At Paignton, the level crossing at Sands Road will be replaced by the Roundham road bridge which is to be reconstructed; at the Torbay Road end a public subway will replace the existing foot bridge. When in due course a new station is built, a site further south is likely to be chosen. The approach from Dartmouth Road will be opened up and will be shorter than at present. The present station accommodation will be nearly trebled, with four platforms all capable of taking the longest trains. New station buildings including a ticket hall, a parcels office and cloak rooms will be provided on the west side. Separate bridges for passengers and luggage will link all platforms. At Goodrington, the plans provide an important series of sidings for passenger coaches, which at present have to be stabled at Newton Abbot, eight miles away. A new 65-foot turntable for locomotives is to be built. Platforms at these stations are to be extended to the standard length of one thousand feet, more or less.

THE CITY PLAN

To the town-planner, few buildings in a modern city are more important than the railway station. Its physical extent bulks large in the city plan. It is the main gateway through which the majority of travellers enter and leave the town. This great concentration of traffic requires broader and more conspicuous road approaches than any other public building. Of such a building it may be said that a perfectly planned town should be grouped around it as the spokes of a wheel are grouped around the hub. Unfortunately, it has generally happened that the railway station was admitted into the cities because it was an inescapable necessity, but only at the price of being hemmed in on every side by narrow streets and jostled by gloomy buildings.

In another chapter we shall be considering the new opportunities for developing town planning in relation to railways and railway stations which are opened up by the Government's programme for new towns. Elsewhere, similar opportunities may occur in connection with schemes for large-scale reconstruction. In some cases the destruction caused by enemy bombing has made such rebuilding an immediate necessity. The City of London is an outstanding example. But among all the towns that suffered in the bombing, there are very few where the railway station falls within the area thrown open for redevelopment. Plymouth is one of these exceptional places. The Great Western is fortunate in being associated with the replanning schemes which the energetic leaders of this great city have lost no time in setting on foot.

Except in the City of London, nothing like the devastation of central Plymouth by enemy bombing has been seen in this country. Forty churches were destroyed with many public buildings and thousands of homes; the damage is said to be equal to one-third of the city's property value. The Great Western bore its share of the loss. Between 10 July, 1940, and 16 November, 1943, the Railway counted 168 air raid incidents on its properties in the Plymouth area. By a miracle the main North Road station escaped with only minor damage, but at the height of the attacks on 22 and 23 April, 1941, great fires destroyed Millbay goods depot, important offices, workshops and sheds at Plymouth Docks, and part of Millbay passenger station. The passenger service to Millbay was suspended and its passenger station has been used for essential goods traffic ever since.

NEXT STATION

PLYMOUTH OF THE FUTURE

There is much to be rebuilt at Plymouth, and the rebuilding will be fitted into the City Council's general plan, an ambitious one which has been fully described in the official publication *A Plan for Plymouth*. The city already has its great dockyard, and its shopping centre for two counties will now be further enlarged by the absorption of the main shopping centre in Devonport. The plan envisages further developments. More is to be made of Plymouth's unique attractions as a holiday resort, which combine the wildness of Dartmoor with some of the most graceful seaboard landscapes in the country. At the projected Atlantic terminal near Millbay Docks, visitors from overseas will be tempted to step ashore in increasing numbers. The new importance of the city is to be expressed in a rebuilt central section which will cut clean across the network of ancient streets and alleys.

The main axis of the new city centre is a straight line drawn between North Road station and the Hoe. The station, according to the authors of the plan, "fits in well with the new plan. . . ." Plymouth has the opportunity for one of the finest railway stations and entrances in the Kingdom, a station that would look up at "a great view across the shopping and civic centre to the naval war memorial on the Hoe," to which it would be linked by a series of lawns and terraces with flights of steps between them. Such are the broad lines on which Plymouth intends to model itself in the future.

The designs for North Road station prepared before the war under the Railways (Agreement) Act, 1935, provided for the whole of the passenger traffic then dealt with at the Millbay and Mutley stations to be concentrated there. All the plans for station buildings, however, will now have to be recast.

Extensive works are also planned for the port of Plymouth, where Millbay Docks are owned and managed by the Great Western. The new Millbay Docks station and luggage warehouse will be worthy of the important passenger traffic from the Atlantic liners now making use of this port. The railway facilities are to be improved and new sidings will be built to keep pace with post-war developments. These schemes, together with the new transit sheds planned for North Quay and Glasgow Wharf, will cost altogether well over half a million pounds.

It will be seen that there is already a remarkable degree of harmony between the Great Western's scheme for the improvement of its system and the City Council's vision of Plymouth of the future. The fusion of these schemes in the gradual shaping of the new town will be watched with interest by town planners all over the world.

THE END OF THE ROAD

One day, when Plymouth, Oxford, Birmingham and many another Great Western city have seen their new stations brought into successful operation, it will be London's turn. That Paddington station must one day be rebuilt is certain. That many will miss the old Paddington of Brunel and Wyatt and Paxton, with its aisles and transepts and its slim wrought iron arabesques, is equally certain. London will be the poorer for its passing; yet London requires that it must go. Fortunately, or unfortunately, the rebuilding of Paddington is not likely to take place for many years to come. The operation will be delayed not only because of its magnitude and its difficulty, which are immense, but also because of all the big London stations Paddington is the one least in need of replanning. The new plan for London as envisaged by the Railway (London Plan) Committee provides for most of the great terminal stations to be re-sited and rearranged. The fact that it was found unnecessary to make any such recommendation in respect of Paddington is a testimony to the matchless skill and foresight of Isambard Kingdom Brunel, its chief creator.

Much may happen, and doubtless will happen, during the years that must elapse before the rebuilding of Paddington can be launched. It is not possible, therefore, to do more in these pages than to indicate in broad outline the facilities which it is thought that the new station may have to offer if it is to fulfil its function in the Great Western system of the future.

The original Paddington station as completed in 1854 contained ten main-line tracks, of which three on the western side of the station were served by departure platforms and two on the eastern side by arrival platforms. The tracks ran close up to the Great Western Hotel and there was nothing corresponding to the main concourse of to-day. Since the last major improvements, which were completed in 1933 at a cost of two million pounds, the station has presented a very different appearance. There are now sixteen platforms in all, of which twelve are situated in the main line station and four in the so-called Suburban station in Bishop's Bridge Road. Of the twelve main-line platforms, only eight abut on the central concourse or circulating area bearing the time-hallowed name of The Lawn. Of these, five serve departing trains, two departing and arriving trains, and one arrivals only.

It will probably be necessary in the new Paddington for main-line trains to be served by a number of platforms equal to the total number now serving both main-line and suburban trains, which is sixteen. To accommodate this larger main-line station, the traffic in parcels and perishable goods now dealt with on the east side of the station would be transferred elsewhere, and the Suburban station also would have to be moved. Incidentally, the underground suburban station suggested in the Report laid before the Government in May, 1946, by the Railway (London Plan) Committee would enable more suburban lines to be projected from Paddington to other parts of London; at the moment the only tracks running through in this manner are the two tracks of the Hammersmith and City Line of the Metropolitan Railway.

That there must be a larger and finer public concourse to match the new scale of the main-line station goes without saying. But of the shape of that concourse, of its position and the position of the new booking hall and other essential parts of the station, it is too early to speak. The problem of finding the necessary space is not made easier by the fact that the Great Western Hotel, as those who have stayed there can testify, has now been turned into one of the most up-to-date and most convenient hotels in London. No doubt the station planners would be glad to see it go, but in the present circumstances its disappearance seems highly unlikely.

How will this new station at Paddington compare with the old, which has served the Railway so well for nearly a century? Brunel's work is a challenge to the architects of to-day. Its planning and lay-out were supreme in its generation. There can be few other big railway stations in this or any other country the main structure of which have successfully met all the requirements of the railway for over fifty years as originally designed. To equal that performance, the architects and engineers would have to design for the year 2000 at the earliest. It seems a long way to look ahead; but then the art of looking ahead is one which the people of the Great Western have continued to practise assiduously since the days of their first great constructors. It is their ambition to apply it not only to the replanning of Paddington but to the transformation of all their stations, large and small, during the years to come.

CHAPTER SEVEN · THE SYSTEM

PROBLEMS OF RENEWAL

THE GREAT WESTERN system of 3,800 route miles of railway line is made up of 9,100 miles of single track containing one and a quarter million tons of steel rails, twenty million sleepers, and thirty million tons of ballast. The Railway from the earliest times has taken particular pride in this track. Apart from extensions and additions, the work of renewal went on unceasingly; before the war, the average rate of renewal of complete track (including ballast, sleepers, chairs and rails) was 334 miles each year. The mileage fell steeply during the war; between 1939 and 1945 the average for each year was 250 miles only. The arrears to be made up amount to close on six hundred miles; they involve the laying of 358,000 tons of ballast, 61,750 tons of sleepers and 83,300 tons of rails. Not until a large proportion of this work has been completed will it be possible to abolish the general wartime speed restrictions and to run trains at pre-war speeds again.

Meanwhile, the programme for 1946 included the renewal of 417 miles of track, of which 367 miles were to be completely relaid and fifty miles reconditioned either with new sleepers or new rails. In all, 187,000 cubic yards of ballast, 526,000 sleepers and 33,400 tons of rails were ordered. The total estimated cost was two million pounds. A similar amount has been provided for work to be done in 1947.

The magnitude and urgency of the task are clearly indicated by the fact that the arrears of maintenance which accumulated during the war are estimated at six thousand man-years in all. In the circumstances, much thought has been given to the problem of increasing the effectiveness of the labour employed. The new methods and devices which are being developed will also have the effect of reducing the interference with train services which is inevitable wherever civil engineering work is in progress.

EXTENSIONS

Efficient railway services depend on the track being always kept in perfect condition. The Great Western, however, believes that its services should not only be kept efficient but should steadily improve in quality. Such improvement involves constant extension of the existing track accommodation. New lengths of track may be required

73

for a variety of purposes, some of which were examined in the previous chapter. Generally speaking, they serve either to simplify a journey by taking a short cut, or to provide separate lines for express traffic so that the number of both express and slow trains may be increased. In the period from 1921 to 1939, the total amount of running track (i.e. excluding sidings) added to the Great Western system for both these purposes amounted to 1,370 miles in all, or more than a quarter of the track existing at the beginning of the period.

The developments at Birmingham, Reading, Bath and Swindon have already been referred to, and others in Swansea and other parts of South Wales will be mentioned elsewhere. In many of these places the additional tracks may either run through the station or round it, and the choice of the most economical and efficient method may present a difficult problem. At Swindon, for example, opinions at the moment are divided on the urgency of additional track accommodation; if the necessity is accepted, the difficulty of running additional tracks through the station is such that the extra tracks would probably take the form of an avoiding line. The plans for such a line show nine miles of completely new track skirting the town of Swindon on the south.

As a rule, however, it is found simpler to add to the tracks in the existing station. A case in point is the tentative plan which has been drawn up for a new and enlarged station at Teignmouth. The Exeter-Newton Abbot section of the line is carrying an increasing burden of traffic, and four tracks have been built at a number of points. For some time, the double track along the coast by way of Dawlish and Teignmouth, which carries the trains to Torquay as well as those for Plymouth and beyond, has been barely sufficient for the greatly expanded Devon and Cornwall traffic. Unfortunately, the configuration of the site does not easily lend itself to the building of additional track; moreover, coast erosion necessitates much repair work which is liable to interfere with services. Plans were accordingly prepared before the war for a new line which was to by-pass Dawlish and Teignmouth, passing under Haldon Down well to the north. The scheme, however, is one of those where the very great amount of work involved, and the rising trend of post-war construction costs, have caused a review to be made of possible alternatives. A new and simpler plan for relieving the pressure on this part of the system provides for the quadrupling of the track in Teignmouth station. Such an arrangement would allow express trains to pass through while stopping trains are standing in the station. The advantages of this smaller scheme do not compare with those of the new line absolutely, but they are probably greater in relation to the estimated cost.

TRACK PROGRAMMES

A number of these track improvements are part of a programme authorised by the Government under the Railways (Agreement) Act, 1935. This Act made possible the construction of a number of new lines and loops, the rebuilding and enlargement

of certain stations, marshalling yards, goods depots and carriage sheds, and the introduction of various improvements in the track and the signalling system designed to
increase the speed, efficiency and safety of train services.

The plans include the doubling of track on the Porthcawl Branch and the Pyle
West Loop in South Wales. Another project which will prove particularly useful to the
operating departments is the modernisation of the Cannock Road coach depot at
Wolverhampton. Generally, the whole of the programme is as necessary to-day as it
was on the day it was drawn up, and the bulk of the work is being dealt with as a matter
of high priority.

The only other improvements ranking with this programme are those authorised
under another Act passed in 1935, the London Passenger Transport (Agreement) Act
to which some reference is made below. It was contemplated at the time these two
Acts came into force that the bulk of the work would be completed by the end of 1940.
The Government have arranged for the financial facilities provided by these Acts to
be extended until such time as the work can be completed. Meanwhile, experts are
reviewing both programmes in every detail. An eleven-year interval is bound to bring
changes in local circumstances; the changes generally may be expected to be all the
greater because the Railway was on war service for more than half that time. Moreover, the greatly increased cost of labour and materials will mean that many of the
schemes may have to be curtailed so that the total expenditure may be kept within the
limit of cost originally provided for.

Additional tracks are still required at a number of points not covered by the 1935
programme, and preparations for some of this work are well advanced. The most
important scheme is that for the completion of a quadruple track without a break
from Paddington to Wootton Bassett in Wiltshire, where the South Wales section
branches off from the Bristol line. Most of this central section of the line has been
quadrupled in instalments at various times; the latest portion to be done was the four-
mile stretch between Wantage Road and Challow, which was completed in 1931. The
present programme for laying additional tracks from Steventon to Wantage Road and
from Challow through Swindon to Wootton Bassett will complete the eighty-three miles
of continuous quadruple track which was envisaged many years ago. The Great
Western will then have the longest stretch of quadruple track in Great Britain; the
longest extant at the moment of writing is the 75-mile line between St. Pancras and
Glendon North Junction on the L.M.S.

A large new holiday camp at Pen-y-Chain (between Pwllheli and Criccieth) in
Caernarvon was completed just before the war. It will be open to the public at Easter,
1947. To serve this camp, a new station has been built to replace the existing Pen-y-
Chain halt; in place of a single line there will be a new double line to connect this station
with Afonwen Junction, where the Great Western system is linked with that of the

A NEW SUBURBAN STATION

FOR LONDON

L.M.S. The full scheme, which will be completed later, includes a larger four-line station and the doubling of the line west of Pen-y-Chain to Pwllheli.

GREATER LONDON

Great Western track extensions are being planned not only to improve existing services but to allow new services to be added where necessary. For example, shortly after the formation of the London Passenger Transport Board in 1933, the Standing Joint Committee of the main-line railways and the Board undertook a searching review of London's passenger transport requirements. To satisfy the most pressing needs, a comprehensive programme was drawn up which included, among other schemes, the extension of the Central Line of the Board's Underground system from North Acton westwards. The entire programme was to be financed by a Government guaranteed loan for which provision was made in the London Transport (Agreement) Act, 1935.

The new Central Line extension was to be built by the Great Western along the south side of the Birmingham main line. The new facilities were intended to serve the considerable housing and industrial developments in this region, more especially those between Park Royal and Greenford. Considerable progress had been made at the outbreak of war with the eight and three-quarter miles to Ruislip. The work was interrupted by the war, but it was resumed on the section to Greenford in the spring of 1946, the Government having indicated their wish to see the work completed with the least possible delay.

Seven new stations will be built at Hanger Lane, Perivale, Greenford, Northolt, South Ruislip, Ruislip Gardens and West Ruislip. All will be of modern layout and design with spacious ticket halls and island platforms 440 feet long and capable of accommodating eight-car trains. A view of a typical station is given on the opposite page. Greenford will be an interchange station where a bay line will accommodate the steam line railcars operating to and from Ealing Broadway. The electric line platforms at Greenford will be thirty-three feet above road level and will be reached by way of escalators. The new lines include a fly-under bridge at North Acton to avoid the Ealing line and adjacent factory buildings, a viaduct over the river Brent at Brentham, lattice girder bridges and concrete fly-over viaducts at Greenford to avoid the east and west curves of the Greenford triangle, and a lattice girder bridge spanning the Grand Union Canal.

The Underground's new car depot constructed between Ruislip Gardens and West Ruislip Station has access at both ends and is capable of stabling about one hundred and fifty cars. Provision will be made for extending the capacity to three hundred cars if this should become necessary at any time in the future. In addition, the existing depot at Wood Lane has been extended to accommodate approximately two hundred cars. Power will be supplied from four sub-stations built at Brentham, Greenford, Northolt and Ruislip. The increased service on the section between Wood Lane and North Acton will be met by increasing the capacity of the existing sub-station at Old Oak Common.

The work is being done in two stages. The first stage will enable services to be projected from North Acton to Greenford, with trains operated from the Wood Lane depot; the second stage will carry the extension to West Ruislip and will bring the Ruislip depot into use.

These schemes for the Greater London region are pre-war schemes. Their necessity is now universally accepted. New plans have been worked out during the war and after, about which it may be said that they certainly point to problems that will require some kind of a solution before many years have passed. Special mention must be made of the revolutionary proposals put forward in the Report of the Railway (London Plan) Committee. These proposals provide for certain suburban trains now terminating at Paddington to be carried in an underground tunnel as far as London Bridge, where a new station known as Tower Bridge Road station would be built. From there the trains would be projected over the suburban system of the Southern Railway into Surrey and Kent. It will be for the Government to decide whether the Railway (London Plan) Committee are right in the view that their scheme "is the smallest that can be devised to serve both its purposes at once – that is, to relieve London's traffic necessities and also to make a substantial contribution to replanning." If the answer is in the affirmative there will be great things to be done.

NEW TOWNS FOR OLD

The London region is not the only place where the Great Western may be called upon to expand its present system. Since the publication in 1940 of the Report of the Royal Commission on the Distribution of the Industrial Population (popularly known as the Barlow Report) the country has gradually come to accept a policy of national planning that will call for important developments in transport and other public services. The latest expression of this policy is to be found in the scheme for establishing a number of new towns which is being developed by the Ministry of Town and Country Planning largely along the lines suggested by the New Towns Committee under the Chairmanship of Lord Reith.

The Minister of Town and Country Planning has stated that "so far as can at present be foreseen, the immediate programme contemplates the creation of some twenty new towns, which includes major extensions of existing towns, in England and Wales. . . . The population in these towns will range between 30,000 and 60,000." At the moment of writing no decisions have been announced in regard to new towns to be created on the Great Western system. It will be recalled, however, that the Greater London Plan prepared by Sir Patrick Abercrombie on Government instructions recommended the establishment of two such towns in the County of Berkshire, one at White Waltham and one at Didcot. Both these sites are on the Great Western main line to Bristol and the west. The Government have declared themselves against a new town at White Waltham; Didcot, fifty-three miles from Paddington, is still a possibility.

The Final Report of the New Towns Committee suggests a population of up to 80,000 for a new town, including its outlying areas falling within a ten-mile radius. The average size of such a town might well be equal to that of, say, Gloucester or Cheltenham. Once a new town is established its growth would be rapid; the New Towns Committee proposes that in the first stage of the development the object of the promoters should be to reach a population of 15,000 to 20,000 in the shortest possible time. It is estimated that the annual increase in accommodation may, under the most favourable circumstances, be sufficient for an intake of between roundly 3,500 and 5,000 persons a year. If this rate of growth can be reached, the first stage should be completed in about four years from the time of starting. We have seen in the previous chapter how the proper placing of the railway and of the railway station in the modern city plan is already being studied in the rebuilding of the central portion of Plymouth. In the new towns yet to be designed, this important problem will be approached at the same time as that of the city plan itself. The result should be something new in British railway history.

The Greater London Plan proposes not only the establishment of new towns but the expansion of existing smaller towns in the same process of decentralisation. The town of Slough, nineteen miles from Paddington, is one of those selected for this purpose. The population of Slough would increase, if these proposals are given effect, by roundly 30,000 or 40,000 to a total of between 100,000 and 110,000. As far as Slough is concerned, the Government have announced their acceptance of this proposal, and have stated their desire that the town of Slough should prepare a civic development plan that will make it worthy of its new status and function, which will be that appropriate to a town somewhat larger in size than Reading or York. Suggestions of a similar kind have been made in regard to Newbury, another Great Western town, but these at the moment of writing remain a matter of speculation.

The effect of the new policy of decentralisation on the development of South Wales is referred to in another chapter. On every side it is clear that the new era of positive town and country planning will throw many fresh burdens on the Great Western system. It is a system that has so far been spared the more unpleasant consequences of rapid and untidy industrial expansion. From now on, the regions it serves will undergo many changes, and in some there will take place a great and remarkable growth. In that growth the Railway is preparing to take a part befitting its long and honourable record in the service of the public.

FACILITIES FOR INDUSTRY

Over and above the essential additions and extensions required for the better operation of ordinary train services, the engineering departments look forward to a considerable programme of minor track construction work designed for the benefit of individual customers, both large and small. A recent example is the work carried out in connection with the new power stations built on behalf of the Central Electricity Board. Anticipating a greatly increased demand for electricity, the Board some time ago embarked on a programme for new plants in various parts of the country calculated to increase existing generating facilities by some three million kilowatts. In the development of this programme, which it is hoped to bring to completion by 1950, the Great Western, besides carrying thousands of tons of material for extensions to plant at Stourport, Hayle, Newport, Tondu, Portishead and Newton Abbot, has provided many additional wagon sidings at all these points. Entirely new power stations are planned for Bromborough and Burry Port. The magnitude of these undertakings is indicated by the fact that the sidings at Burry Port alone will require a holding capacity of one thousand wagons plus reserve "standage" for empties. Incidentally, the coal consumption of this station will probably be in the region of five thousand tons a day.

Not all the customers requiring special lines and sidings are of the same importance, but on the Great Western system even the humblest receives the same attention as the greatest and most powerful. Arrangements for private sidings are made under the Railways (Private Sidings) Act of 1904; they enable the manufacturer to receive his raw materials in full wagon loads direct into his store, and to load his finished product straight off his conveyor belt into the waiting wagons. The cost of road transport is saved; there are special (and usually very moderate) rates for traffic conveyed over the siding ; labour is economised through the avoidance of double handling; and the need for storage space both for materials and for finished products is reduced to a minimum. Thus the capital cost of the siding is soon recouped. The customer may also save himself much clerical work by adopting the Wagon Standage method for charging costs on the basis of a weekly wagon return (with a substantial free standage allowance) instead of by the normal demurrage system. There are very few industries in this country that are not represented among users of private sidings on the Great Western system, but such sidings are especially useful to collieries, steel works, gas and electricity undertakings and others that depend on a heavy flow of bulky material entering or leaving the works. They are certain to play a conspicuous part in the great industrial expansion that is now taking place in various parts of the country, more particularly in the South Wales region.

ENGINEERING TECHNIQUE

In the planning of these new works and improvement schemes with their bridges and other ancillary structures, modern scientific methods are being increasingly used by all Great Western engineers. It is not possible in these pages to do more than mention a few of the new developments in this department. They will serve to illustrate a trend that is certain to show an impressive advance in speed, efficiency and economy during the years to come.

New construction starts below ground level. In dealing with foundation problems, uncertainty is avoided by the use of the modern science of soil mechanics. Methods of testing have been developed with the co-operation of the Soil Mechanics Section of the Building Research Station of the Department of Scientific and Industrial Research. These methods are particularly useful where structures are to be built on a poor quality subsoil such as clay. Where the foundations rest on rock or gravel, there is little doubt about the capacity to carry loads, but where clay is encountered the carrying capacity of the ground cannot be ascertained from a casual inspection, or even from trial loading. Clays may be identical in appearance, but tests will disclose very widely varying properties. The usual procedure is to sink a four-inch thick steel tube thirty or more feet into the ground and to make a detailed examination of the material brought up through the tube. Where clay strata are encountered, a thin metal cylinder is thrust down the tube into the clay and given a twist, which breaks off a cylindrical clay sample. The cylinder is then withdrawn; the sample obtained, being practically in its natural state, is known as an "undisturbed" sample. Various routine tests are applied to this sample, one of which is a compression test giving a direct indication of the load that the clay will bear.

The science of soil mechanics is used not only to obtain the data necessary for the design of new structures but to diagnose and cure failures or incipient failures in existing engineering works such as embankments, cuttings or bridges.

For all types of bridges which in the past were built of steel or of concrete poured *in situ*, the Great Western is developing new methods of design based on the use of reinforced pre-cast concrete units. Concurrently, a programme of research and experiment has been undertaken with a view to establishing the most satisfactory forms of surface treatment. In new overbridges or footbridges of moderate span, the concrete superstructure is in reinforced concrete pre-cast units. Overbridges up to about thirty feet span are built with concrete joists wherever suitable construction depth is available. In existing underbridges, flat concrete slabs are being used extensively to replace timber or metal decks due for renewal. Several long aqueducts and an engine shed have recently been constructed in reinforced concrete units. Reinforced concrete is also being used for standard station canopies, warehouses, and other structures.

NEXT STATION

PREFABRICATION OF TRACK

But perhaps the most interesting development in Great Western engineering is the prefabrication or pre-assembly of track complete with rails and sleepers.

The standard practice for laying track is to put down sleepers on the prepared ballast at specified intervals, and afterwards to place each rail in position and secure it to the sleepers. With the new method, the rails and sleepers are framed up together in an assembly yard and loaded into wagons as complete track units. Successive units are unloaded and put down by the use of mobile cranes. The old, *in-situ* method of laying sleepers and rails required on an average 1,400 man-hours per mile of track; it is estimated that the pre-assembly method will reduce the figure to one thousand man-hours, a saving of close on one-third in the use of man-power. Since the total period for which a line must be closed for traffic will average nine hours as compared with twenty-four with the old, track occupancy by maintenance gangs is likely to be reduced by something like sixty per cent. The new method, however, requires the use of two tracks instead of one as formerly, so that its application will necessarily be limited by conditions at the site.

A new method is also being tried for fastening track direct to the reinforced concrete deck of bridges. This does away with sleepers and ballast and allows additional depth for the supporting steelwork girders. In this design, the rail chairs are laid direct on the pre-cast reinforced concrete slab deck.

An essential part of prefabrication of track is the provision of assembly depots at a number of places on the system. One, and possibly more, of these depots will also have facilities for welding rails. The welding of rails was first undertaken some years before the war. The added comfort to the traveller is an important advantage with the welded rail, but there is also a considerable saving in maintenance work as compared with the old form of track. The intention is to weld together anything up to five standard length rails into a single unit. Unfortunately, the most up-to-date method of rail welding, the so-called "flash butt" process, cannot be applied to *in-situ* work on the line. The depot which it is proposed to equip with plant using this process will be capable of welding together five rails to make one rail three hundred feet long. At this and other depots, facilities are to be provided for dismantling old track recovered from relaying, the materials being sorted and sent out for re-use or sold as scrap.

In all track construction, considerable progress has been made with the flat bottom rail, of which much experience has now been gained. This rail is similar to the standard bull-head rail except for the fact that the bottom flange which supports the rail is more than double the width – $5\frac{3}{4}$ inches instead of $2\frac{3}{4}$. The rail is, therefore, considerably stiffer than the bull-head type. Instead of cast-iron chairs to carry the rail, base plates are used, with elastic spikes holding the rail and base plate to the sleeper. By the beginning of 1947, flat bottom rails had been fixed on forty miles of main-line track. Though the initial cost is somewhat higher than for the standard type, maintenance costs will be less and the new track is expected to have a longer life. If these extended trials prove successful, the new type rail will be increasingly used in the regular programmes for track renewal as well as in new construction.

NEW TOOLS AND PLANT

New tools and equipment will help to give extra speed to the types of work here described. Much use will be made of the Railway's expanding fleet of mechanical excavators, angle dozers, concrete mixers, caterpillar tractors, air compressors, cranes, hoists, winches, tipping wagons, pumps, pile drivers, power rammers, power picks, road sweepers and road rollers. Travelling cranes will be employed more extensively for removing and relaying tracks, and mechanised shovels and conveyors will load yard refuse and other materials into wagons. Power-driven tools are being used in increasing number for many different operations, where necessary in conjunction with mobile power units capable of driving up to four tools simultaneously. The source of power may be either electricity or compressed air. Other tools inject cement grout into ballast foundations where these require to be strengthened. The same pressure grouting tools will also expel accumulations of water and so reduce the extent of drainage work required.

An interesting new machine is being provided at refuse tipping sites for unloading wagons, so that manpower may be released for other work. A plate travels to and fro along the jib of this machine and, when the plate is put into the wagon, it forces out the contents through the door on the far side. The machine can also be used to slew the track of the tip siding and can push wagons along the siding if necessary. Another very simple tool has been devised for forcing pipes into wet banks and cutting slopes to drain off water pockets, giving additional stability; yet another type is put into man-holes to force rods into choked drains. There is a tool which, when connected to a steam cock of an engine, may be used for directing jets of steam into points clogged by ice or snow. Machines will also dispose of such lineside jobs as trimming edges, cutting grass, and ploughing strips alongside hedges, timber fences, etc., to act as fire breaks.

These new power-operated and other tools will considerably lessen the physical toil required of the men who work on the railway. They will also remind the men who use them that the old standards of quality and efficiency have not been lowered but, if anything, have been raised higher still. "In forming all my plans," wrote Brunel in one of his earliest reports, "I have looked to the perfection of the surface on which the carriages are to run as the great and ultimate desideratum." Travellers in Great Western trains can testify that his words are not forgotten by those to whom it has fallen to maintain, improve and extend the great work of his life.

CHAPTER EIGHT · SIGNALLING

SAFETY FIRST

THE railways of Great Britain are not given to boasting of their remarkable safety record. Nevertheless, this record is known and envied all the world over. Between 1923 and 1945, the chances of getting killed as a result of a railway accident in Great Britain were seventy-five million to one against. Such a record is a striking tribute to the alert mind and the cool judgment of the railwaymen in charge of tracks, trains and signals. It is no less a testimony to the reliability of the equipment to which several generations of railway engineers have given their best inventive thought.

Among the people of the Great Western it has long been realised that, while the possibility of human error can be minimised, it can never be eliminated altogether. Forty years ago – in January, 1906 – the Railway's scientists and engineers started to experiment with a device designed to give a maximum of protection against the possibility of mistakes. The device, which has become famous under the name of Automatic Train Control, covers only a section of the field of possible human error, but it is a section of crucial importance. It has been estimated by Government experts that on lines not equipped with Automatic Train Control, out of every hundred accidents into which official enquiries were held (i.e. accidents involving loss of life or other serious consequences), twelve or thirteen would have been prevented if this system had been installed.

In 1931, the Great Western took advantage of the facilities provided by the Development (Loan Guarantees and Grants) Act, 1929, to equip with Automatic Train Control 2,500 locomotives and 2,130 miles of main line track from Paddington to Plymouth, Fishguard and Shrewsbury. The system more than justified itself. The remaining sections of the track were put in hand in 1938, and when war broke out the work was practically finished. On 9 November, 1939, the last piece of equipment was installed at Penzance. By this time, 3,250 locomotives had been fitted, and 2,114 installations fixed over 2,852 miles of track.

The Automatic Train Control installation is one of the most advanced safety devices in use on any railway. It is not fully automatic to the extent of turning the driver into a mechanic travelling in a robot train. Such a robot train is used in this country only by the Post Office for the carriage of mails; this train has neither driver nor passengers. Railway engineers would have little difficulty in designing an automatic passenger train if they were called upon to do so; for the present, however, it is clear that the public prefers that trains shall be in the charge of a human driver. The question of the proper scope of Automatic Train Control, and of the degree to which the driver's responsibilities should be curtailed, is one to which careful study has been given not only by the Railway itself but by the Government Committee set up in 1927 to report upon the subject. The principle was finally laid down by the Government that it should be the object of Automatic Train Control to reproduce inside the locomotive cab the indication given by each distant signal as the train moves forward on its journey.

Most people are aware that it is the purpose of a distant signal to give advance warning to the driver that he may find one or several stop signals against him. The signal normally precedes a stop signal by the estimated braking distance of the train, which may be eight hundred yards, more or less. It is distinguished by a signal arm painted yellow and having a swallow-tail end; the colour light indication is also yellow. When a caution signal is "on," the driver must at once reduce speed so that he may pull up promptly if the following stop signal should require him to do so. This is the type of signal with which Great Western Automatic Train Control is linked. The Train Control track apparatus is usually fixed a little over four hundred yards from the distant signal.

AUTOMATIC TRAIN CONTROL IN ACTION

The Automatic Train Control as used by the Great Western goes far beyond the primary function of reproducing a signal on the train. Its purpose is twofold. First, it tells the driver, by means of aural signals inside his cab, what is the position of the distant signal ahead. The train, therefore, is fully protected in cases where bad visibility or momentary inattention on the driver's part may have caused the signals to be overlooked. In the second place, where a driver has heard the "caution" signal indication but for some reason fails or is unable to take the correct action, the Automatic Train Control will apply the brakes and pull up the train. A number of devices are in use on electric railways which achieve one or both of these objects. The London Underground, for example, has an installation which has proved its worth over a period of years. On an electric railway the electrical circuit provides a simple and effective means of controlling the movements of trains. The Great Western installation is chiefly remarkable for having applied similar methods to much more difficult conditions of steam train operation. The efficacy of the automatic braking device has been shown in a series of public demonstrations. The most recent of these took place just before the war. A train weighing 430 tons, including the engine and tender, and travelling at a speed of about sixty miles an hour, was pulled up "against the steam" in nine hundred yards. As the device was installed on the track at a distance of 1,350 yards from the stop signal, it will be seen that the margin of safety was a substantial one.

The aural signals are a bell for the clear indication which corresponds with the "off" position of the signal arm, and a siren which warns the driver that the signal is in the "on" position. The positive indication for a clear signal is an invaluable safeguard in that it will automatically detect a fault or failure in the apparatus. The driver knows that at every appropriate point he should hear either one or the other of the signals; if he fails to hear the bell he will know that something is wrong, and, if necessary, will pull up his train. A second detective device is provided by the fact that the caution indication is given not by switching on an electric current but by switching it off. Any fault in the electrical circuit, therefore, must necessarily result in a caution indication; the siren would sound and the train would be brought to a stop.

In one official report after another, tributes have been paid to the brilliant performance of this device. Railway experts in all parts of the world have studied it in the closest detail. The special Government Committee was greatly impressed with its value. The Government's Chief Inspector of Railways, in a recent report, reiterates and endorses the views expressed by that Committee. He speaks of "the necessity for providing equipment designed to give positive assistance to the footplate staff in obeying signal instructions," in other words, that form of "Automatic Train Control which was described by the Automatic Train Control Committee in 1930 as a 'direct' means for improving security and preventing train accidents, in comparison with the 'indirect' methods of facilitating the task of drivers by improving the display and lighting of signals themselves. As was pointed out in the Committee's Report, the latter methods are very valuable for assisting drivers to observe and obey signals, but they are not positive preventives, and in this respect are inferior from the safety aspect to 'direct' methods of linking wayside signals with the footplate."

Automatic Train Control was introduced as a safety device, but in practice it has proved to be much more than that. The aural signals provide direct communication between the signalman and the locomotive crew. Since the driver is no longer entirely dependent on the signals at the side of the track, he can proceed with absolute confidence whatever the state of the weather. The strain and tension of driving in fog and snow are eased, and speed is maintained without difficulty. The apparatus is used not only as a warning device but as a position indicator when visibility is poor. As one bell ring follows another, the driver is constantly aware of the exact location of his train. The Automatic Train Control has played a special part in the development of the Great Western express goods trains, most of which run during the night. The low cost of the installation – less than £100 per mile of track before the war, including the locomotive equipment – is another striking advantage. The cost of maintenance was about £10 per mile per annum. When it is considered that other safety devices, like colour light signalling, cost anything up to £5,000 per mile of track before the war, it will be seen how outstandingly economical is the Great Western system in relation to the results achieved. The equipment at the end of 1946 included 3,364 installations on loco-motives and 2,462 control ramps on the track.

TRACK CIRCUITING

At about the same time as the earliest experiments with Automatic Train Control, Great Western engineers introduced another safety device of the highest importance in which the electrification of the track is used for a variety of purposes. This device is generally known under the name of track circuiting. The electrical current in this case does not pass through a separate ramp but through a section of the actual track rails which is insulated at each end from the rest of the track. Here are some of the things the track circuit device does: it tells the signalman whether there is a train in the circuited section between two signal boxes; it makes it impossible for the clear signal to be given while there is a train in this section; in conjunction with power-operated points it enables the area controlled from a signal box to be extended indefinitely; it "holds" the route ahead and automatically prevents points being moved by accident or carelessness while a train is approaching or passing over them; and it may also be made to replace the signals to "danger" after the train has passed, and lock them firmly in that position.

The first track circuit on the Great Western was installed in 1907 at Basildon, between Pangbourne and Goring. In October, 1945, the number of track circuit installations on the Company's system was 4,672 altogether. This is equivalent to roundly five track circuits to every four route miles of track; yet year by year this instal-lation still continues to grow. It is hoped that during the five year period from 1946 to 1950 many more track circuits will be added. Track circuiting saves labour as well as giving additional safety. Between 1930 and 1945 it made it possible for 115 minor signal boxes to be dispensed with; another forty boxes are to be abolished under the post-war programme. To some extent the work done in these boxes is transferred to other more centrally situated boxes.

SIGNALLING OF THE FUTURE

During the war, experiments were made with certain improvements and simpli-fications which made the Automatic Train Control installation even more absolutely dependable. The most important change is in the method for operating the "clear" signal. In its original form the apparatus was worked by electrical current supplied by an accumulator. In 1932, a modified design was introduced in which the installation was operated mechanically in conjunction with the electrical impulses received from the ramp on the track. Further improvements in this electro-mechanical apparatus are now being examined and tested. In the newest type, the accumulator is eliminated from the locomotive installation; this equipment generally is simpler and sturdier and can be manufactured at less cost. The new type of apparatus has been installed on a number of locomotives so that it may be fully tested under normal service conditions before it is standardised for general use.

This and other improvements in detail, however valuable they may be, do not affect the general performance of the Automatic Train Control as it exists to-day. The engineers of the Great Western, however, are experimenting with entirely new developments which will increase the scope and flexibility of the device so that it may be linked with any method of signalling, in this or any other country, including the most complex.

The audible indications now given by the Automatic Train Control are two in number, and of these two only one is an indication of danger or impending danger. Exhaustive tests and experiments led the Railway to link this indication with the distant or caution signal. Experience proved them to be right. The next problem to be attacked was to provide a third aural indication which would make it possible for the driver of a train to receive a separate indication for each aspect of more elaborate signalling systems.

Travellers on suburban railway lines are familiar with signalling systems in which there are four colour light indications instead of three. These more elaborate signals are necessary on lines where a close succession of trains run at varying speeds with varying powers of acceleration and braking. The elaboration consists as a rule of a second caution signal, so that there are separate caution signals for fast and slow trains, each placed in its appropriate position along the line. The first of these signals to be encountered is that addressed to the fast train; this signal is also useful in providing a preliminary warning to the slow train. The second caution signal is intended for the slow train only. Under exceptional conditions, still further visual indications may be found necessary; a five-aspect installation is actually working on a short section of line in this country. The Automatic Train Control of the future will reproduce in the driver's cab these and any other aspects or indications which may be adopted for railway signalling. Where necessary, it will substitute for the continuous electrical current in the track a series of separate electrical impulses, using a different pattern of impulses for each indication. Thus the Automatic Train Control will become a complete signalling system which would be capable (if such a thing should ever be seriously considered) of taking over the whole of the signalling operations now performed by fixed signals erected along the track.

INTO THE ETHER

Scientific research in signalling matters is not confined to the improvement of existing devices. The possibilities of radio and radar, for example, are being studied with the utmost care. Great Western engineers are closely following the many schemes in which the striking wartime development of these two devices is being applied to the problems of civil aviation. The process is a slow and painful one, and it is only too obvious that some years will elapse before the work can bear fruit. The Railway believes that the perfected Automatic Train Control will leave little scope for radar devices in railway signalling, but they are not the less anxious to exploit them for whatever purpose they may be able to fulfil.

Radio, again, is being extensively used in some countries for the purpose of establishing communication between the locomotive driver and fixed control points, but its use is restricted to stretches of line where trains are few and signalling installations correspondingly simple. On the Great Western system, radio communication is likely in the near future to be tried out in marshalling yards, where it will enable controllers to send out continuous instructions to drivers. Another use of radio would be to establish telephonic communication between the driver and the guard such as is already provided on London Underground trains by way of an ordinary wired installation. But whether these and other tasks can be performed by radio depends in the last resort on the Government, who have not as yet been able in this country to grant the railways permission to use a wavelength within the suitable range of ether waves.

SIGNALS HEADQUARTERS

The importance attached by the Great Western management to the development of its signalling arrangements is clearly illustrated by the fact that it was the first railway in this country to make the Department of the Signal Engineer an independent organisation of equal rank with the other engineering departments. Since 1897 the Signal Engineer has held the status of a principal officer reporting direct to the management and the Board, and since 1903 he has also been responsible for the whole of the telecommunications system including the elaborate network associated with traffic control. In addition to his 1,843 signal boxes controlling 41,954 signals of all types and sizes, he has the oversight of 73 telephone exchanges connecting 27,200 telephones by way of 65,000 miles of lines and using current from 300,000 batteries.

To meet the needs of a rapidly developing staff watching over £14 million worth of technical apparatus, the whole of the existing signal and telegraph works at Reading are shortly to be rebuilt at a cost of £300,000. The new buildings will include a group of large single-storey workshops connected to a three-storey warehouse block standing at the south-west corner of the site. The largest shop – the erecting shop – will cover a floor area of over 25,000 square feet, and others, like the machine, fitting and carpenters' shops, will vary between 13,000 and 18,000 feet. The warehouse block will contain a telegraph shop and a testing shop for all types of equipment as well

THE NEW SIGNAL WORKS, READING

PRELIMINARY DESIGN 1946

as plentiful storage space. The whole of the ground floors are to be 3 ft. 6 ins. above rail level, which is the level of the loading platform provided on two sides of the building. The total floor area is 150,000 square feet.

While thus laying great emphasis on the business of the Signal Department the Great Western none the less fully recognises the close association that exists between the signal and the track. It is the combination of these two things that produces the perfect railway system; and the Railway has retained the practice of bringing them together under a single Engineering Committee of the Board. An American expert has defined the ideal of a railway as a clean, smooth, safe, fast ride. To provide such a ride a railway needs above all a first-class system, and the Great Western's organisation has shown at least one method by which a first-class system may be created and maintained.

CHAPTER NINE · GROWTH OF A REGION

THE GREAT WESTERN AND SOUTH WALES

A SPECIAL place in this account must be given to the Great Western's plans for South Wales. For many years the Railway has been linked to South Wales by the closest ties. The region has 3,265 miles of railway lines served by 445 Great Western passenger stations and halts. The great South Wales ports on the Bristol Channel are owned and managed by the Great Western. The important Great Western steamship services to Ireland are based on a South Wales port, and other steamship services from Weymouth to the Channel Islands come under the control of the Welsh central office. Each year, a substantial proportion of the Railway's total outlay on wages and salaries, on municipal rates and on the purchase of coal, materials and stores, is spent in South Wales. The growth of the Great Western and the growth of industrial South Wales have to a large extent proceeded hand in hand, and the association is likely to continue. It is no accident that this region should occupy a unique position in the Railway's plans for the future.

The wartime history of the South Wales ports is a remarkable one. More than once, leaders of the present Government as well as those of the last have paid tribute to the magnificent contribution to the national effort made by this group of ports at a highly critical period of the war. They have stated the Government's intention of safeguarding the interests of the ports on their return to peacetime trading. The process of reconversion will not be easy. Some disturbing facts were disclosed in a recent Report published by the South Wales and Monmouthshire Joint Ports Committee under the title *Trade Development through the South Wales and Monmouthshire Ports*. It is stated, for example, that the ports owe their modern development largely to the coal export trade, yet "for many years the export of coal has dwindled until, from their peak of nearly forty million tons in one year, the South Wales ports in 1945 dealt with only five million tons." The total volume of exports and imports has also declined, though not in the same proportion. Much of this decline is due to a fall in the output of the Welsh manufacturing industries which provided the principal articles of export in the past. But to some extent the unrestricted competition of other British ports is also responsible.

GREAT WESTERN HOTEL, SWANSEA

PRELIMINARY DESIGN

The Report refers, for example, to "the number of vessels which discharge at other ports large quantities of cargo destined for South Wales and territories well within the influence of the South Wales ports."

The Joint Committee makes a number of suggestions which it is hoped will remedy the present state of affairs. The ports, it says, are well equipped to handle general as well as specialised cargoes. Above all, it maintains that the future prosperity of the region can only be secured if the ports cease to be purely local ports as they have tended to be in the past, and follow the general practice of serving an area "wider than the immediate *hinterland*."

WARTIME BEGINNINGS

The Great Western is fortunate in being able to tackle its improvement programme in South Wales from a flying start, for extensive additions to its system were carried out for military purposes during the war. These include the quadrupling of the 4½ miles of track between Newport and Severn Tunnel Junction, and additional marshalling yards and sidings at most of the Great Western docks, where modern roadways give access to the quaysides independently of the existing rail connections. There are ample transit sheds and warehouses; cranes for handling general cargoes have been provided on a great scale. The cost of these and of dock improvements carried out during the war was considerably more than a million pounds. The result is that, as was recently stated in Parliament, a 10,000-ton general cargo liner can now be dealt with as quickly in Cardiff as in any other great general cargo port in the Kingdom. The port of Cardiff for general cargo purposes is now second to none.

In completing and extending these important improvements, the Great Western intends, so far as possible, to hold the balance equally between the individual ports, so that the maximum benefit may accrue to the group as a whole. Cranes and all equipment that has not been modernised will be quickly dealt with. New electrical machinery will take the place of existing steam-driven impounding pumps and hydraulic pressure pumps. In consultations with the ship-repairing industry, the Great Western proposes to allocate berths at all the ports to be used for ship repairs. Oil separating barges and in some cases sea-water ballasting facilities will be provided at Newport, Cardiff, Barry and Swansea.

WELSH INDUSTRY

Yet however much may be done to bring wider industrial areas within the field served by the South Wales ports, the prosperity of the ports and of South Wales generally can only be assured by a revival of industry in Wales itself. As far as coal production is concerned, it is well known that, at the end of the war, experts held widely divergent views regarding its future prospects. The Great Western, however, has decided to take no chances. Existing facilities for handling coal export cargoes were retained. It is realised that, for the time being, these facilities will be far in excess of current needs. The Railway's policy, however, is that all possible developments in South Wales trade and industry shall be foreseen and provided for as circumstances permit, and the revival of the coal export trade is certainly held to fall within the range of such developments. In the coal markets of the world, South Wales coal still holds its place as one of the finest fuels in existence.

To offset the decline in the heavy industries of South Wales, new industries are being established in many places. During the year 1945, no less than ninety-six new factory schemes submitted to the Government received official approval and support. Most of the schemes are associated with the light industries which South Wales needs to balance its industrial structure. The workers have been quick to learn the new trades. This entrance of new industries is often a cumulative process: one firm entering the area later attracts a number of related concerns. Aberdare Cables, Ltd., for example, were among the first of the new undertakings. In 1937 they built a factory at Aberdare and soon discovered the virtues of Welsh labour. To-day, after an intensive war effort, they produce paper and cambric insulated cables on a large scale. They employ some four hundred workers, mostly men, and hope to increase the number when the world lead shortage improves.

The experience of Aberdare Cables, Ltd., has led to many similar developments elsewhere. The presence of such firms in the development area, and their increasing success, form a very powerful inducement for other firms to enter the area in their turn. A high place in point of size must be given to the plans of British Nylon Spinners, Ltd., who have taken a site of some one million square feet at Manhilad, near Pontypool, and to Monsanto Chemicals, Ltd., who have gone to Newport for their site. The cost of these projects, including plant and factories, will run into many millions of pounds. Industry functioning on this scale is bound to lead to subsidiary undertakings, and some ancillary developments of this nature have already been announced. All these firms, large and small, are providing direct employment and all are customers of other local industries, so that their influence is spreading in a continually widening circle of social and commercial benefits. This transformation of life and work in South Wales is among the most remarkable features of the industrial life of Britain to-day.

The Great Western is actively co-operating with manufacturers and others who have developments in view. There is, for example, the difficult business of industrial location. The scientific study of location problems was initiated many years ago and staff were trained to conduct investigations and deal with industrialists' inquiries. The intelligence service was conducted in conjunction with the Board of Trade and with the co-operation of the Nuffield organisation and other expert bodies. Its value became widely known and its activities multiplied until in 1938 more than seven hundred enquiries were taken up and appropriate sites in various parts of the country were

CROSS-CHANNEL STEAMER

THE THIRD-CLASS LOUNGE

found for a total of sixty-three firms. In South Wales alone, 121 new firms were introduced to the region during the three years 1937-9. To-day the information collected by this organisation, which during the war years was widely used by the British and American Governments, is once more at the disposal of industrial firms; new information is constantly being added to the existing store.

The new industries making their home in South Wales will require a considerable expansion of the services provided by the Great Western and other great utilities. New railway lines and many miles of new sidings will have to be built. New road transport services will be required, as, for example, at Hirwaun and Bridgend, where new trading estates converted out of wartime Ordnance Factories depend on Great Western road transport for the despatch of their manufactured goods. The Railway is giving work of this kind the highest degree of priority. The organisation which studies the planning of transport facilities for new industries has a Cardiff office working in close touch with the Board of Trade, and with the chief officers of the Great Western in London.

THE EASTERN SOUTH WALES PORTS

More and more, these new industries will also come to depend for their prosperity on South Wales ports and South Wales ships. The ports, which during the war handled ninety-four million tons of traffic, are fully ready to play their part in building up a strong commercial activity.

Reading from east to west on the map, the principal South Wales ports (all owned by the Great Western) are Newport, Cardiff, Barry, Port Talbot and Swansea. The general improvements to be carried out in all these places have been briefly indicated; reference must now be made to certain individual works which are of special interest.

At Newport an additional transit shed is planned for South Quay. The total cost was estimated some time ago at £120,000, but will no doubt be substantially higher. A number of the latest high capacity cranes are to be provided to equip a special berth for the rapid discharging of iron ore and similar bulk cargoes. The junction passage between the North and South Docks will be deepened and widened to allow of large vessels entering North Dock. New slipways will be built for the quicker and more efficient repair of lock gates. The central workshops attached to the dock will have new fitting and machine shops and the boiler shops will be improved and modernised.

Additions and improvements to transit sheds of 866,000 square feet at the Queen Alexandra and Roath Docks, Cardiff, are estimated to cost £380,000. At these Docks there is also a modern cold store large enough to accommodate 10,000 tons of frozen meat. Up-to-date crane equipment is to be augmented; extensive new sidings on the foreshore will provide improved facilities for the stacking of mining and sawn timber. In consultation with the Association of Ship Owners and Ship Repairers, a study is being made of present and future requirements at the Commercial Dry Dock, one of the three largest dry docks in this port, with a view to the extension of existing ship repair facilities. A new hotel to be built at Cardiff is referred to elsewhere.

At Barry, the Great Western owns the Commercial Graving Docks, 860 feet long. One of the most urgent needs of South Wales at the present moment is the provision of dry docking facilities capable of dealing with the larger types of cargo vessels now being built by the more progressive owners. With the advice of the shipping interests, plans have been prepared which include the widening of the present sixty-foot entrance to a width of 75 feet at an estimated cost of over £400,000. The dock in future will therefore be capable of dealing with vessels of 72 feet 6 inches beam instead of being limited to fifty-five feet beam as at present. Additional equipment is to be installed at the sheds to deal more expeditiously with general cargoes.

The wartime improvements at these three ports include not only transit sheds and other structures, but a considerable number of new electric cranes. Newport has six of these, Cardiff twenty and Barry eighteen. One in four of these new cranes is of the powerful six-ton type.

PORT TALBOT

Further west lie the two important ports of Port Talbot and Swansea. The first of these in particular is likely to be the centre of far-reaching developments. One of the major undertakings envisaged in the post-war plans of the British steel industry is a new hot strip mill to be erected by Guest, Keen & Baldwins Iron and Steel Co., Ltd., near the Margam Works, in Port Talbot. Ancillary cold reduction plants for turning the hot rolled strip into tin plate are planned for Llangefelach and Llanelly, in the Swansea district. The new Port Talbot strip mill with its annual capacity of roundly one million tons will thus be making a vital contribution to the total estimated production of tinplates totalling some twenty million basis boxes a year (of which three-quarters is to be supplied by the big continuous strip mills and the rest from the older works). The new hot strip mill will also produce fully-finished motor-car sheets.

In connection with this great plant the Great Western has a programme of sidings and other improvements estimated to cost £750,000 in all. The works at Margam will cover a distance of about three miles, and will include over one and a half miles of double railway track to the docks; embankments requiring half a million cubic yards of earthworks; a thirteen-arch viaduct 150 yards long; six steel bridges, varying from thirty-three feet to 120 feet span, and six hundred yards of massive retaining walls. The existing Ogmore Vale Extension single line railway will be doubled between Margam Moors and Margam (a distance of one and a half miles) and at either end of this length marshalling yards, each with siding accommodation for approximately a thousand ten-ton wagons, will be provided. In all, nearly twenty miles of single track will be laid down for the new scheme. Road access will necessitate a new overbridge across the existing four lines of railway at the south end of the site and at the north end a new underbridge will be provided. Margam Wharf is also to be extended to permit of two ore vessels being dealt with simultaneously.

Much of the site for the new works is at present marsh land, and a large number of piles will be driven to considerable depth to carry the various structures. New water mains and considerable extensions to the drainage system will also be required. Additions and alterations to existing signal installations, including the provision of two new signal boxes, will involve an expenditure of over £80,000. Port Talbot docks are also to have a large transit shed of the latest type, and a new electric hydraulic power station which with its equipment is estimated to cost £100,000. The railway station will be extensively remodelled and renovated. Incidentally, wartime improvements at Port Talbot include a new berth for oil tankers, the widening by dredging of the approach channel to Steelworks Wharf, and the installation of four new cranes.

SWANSEA

At Swansea the new works are mainly concerned with improved road access to Kings Dock. The scheme is a large one including a new bridge and will cost upwards of £50,000. The electrification of the hydraulic power stations here is a very considerable enterprise. There will be greatly increased storage space estimated to cost £34,000 for export cargoes not requiring covered accommodation. Works completed during the war include a new cargo shed (in addition to reconstructed sheds replacing two which were destroyed in enemy attacks), new berths for general cargoes, and twenty electric cranes; another eleven cranes have since been added, making a total of thirty-one new cranes since 1939.

In the town of Swansea, a scheme is in preparation for extensive improvements of High Street station. A new goods depot will be built in a more central position, planned and equipped to handle large volumes of goods smoothly and with great speed. It is understood that Swansea Corporation have under consideration an ambitious town-planning scheme which may involve the abolition of the low-level railway tracks which now follow the main road and cross the New Cut by the swing bridge. If this scheme should be accepted, these tracks would probably have to be diverted over the high-level railway bridge which now carries the main railway lines at this point.

Whatever may be decided about this last development, it is clear that Swansea is going to be a busy place as far as the Great Western is concerned. There is to be a new hotel with not less than 150 bedrooms (a drawing of the exterior appears on page 93). The existing housing estate for Great Western staff is also to be extended by the building of additional houses.

CROSS-CHANNEL STEAMER

1947

Close to Swansea lies the little seaside town of Porthcawl. Trains to and from Porthcawl now connect at Pyle with the main line trains between Cardiff and Swansea. A double track already exists from Pyle to Cornelly; the programme authorised under the Railways (Agreement) Act, 1935, included the doubling of the track between Cornelly and Porthcawl to carry the expanding traffic to this popular resort. The first instalment, the one and a quarter miles between Cornelly and Nottage, is in hand at the moment of writing. Another improvement planned at that time (1935) was a western loop at Pyle which would enable a through train service to be established between Swansea, Neath and Porthcawl. This loop also will be completed as a matter of urgency.

Concurrently with these improvements to the track, a new station is being planned for Porthcawl itself. The present station lies on the south side of the Station Hill level crossing which the local authority and the townsfolk would like to be abolished. It is hoped that the new station will be so placed that the level crossing may be avoided. It will have four tracks served by two full-length island platforms.

ON THE SEAS

The Great Western has been in the passenger steamship business since 1872, when Parliamentary powers were obtained to take over the regular service between New Milford (afterwards re-named Neyland) and Waterford and Cork which the Railway had caused to be instituted sixteen years earlier. An older service which also owes its inception to the support and encouragement of the Great Western is that which links Guernsey and Jersey with Weymouth; this was not transferred to the Company till 1889. In 1927 the general control of the whole of the Great Western steamship services was placed under the Chief Docks Manager, from whose office at Cardiff they have been managed ever since.

In 1939, in addition to its fleet of cargo boats, passenger tenders and miscellaneous craft, the Railway had six passenger steamships in regular operation. The largest of these were the 2,700-ton vessels in the Fishguard-Rosslare service, of which only one, the *St. Andrew*, has survived its strenuous wartime exploits. The *St. David* was sunk in the Mediterranean and the *St. Patrick* in the Irish Channel. Next in size were the *St. Julien* and the *St. Helier*, each of 1,950 tons and sailing between Weymouth and the Channel Islands. Lastly there was the *Great Western*, of 1,660 tons, sailing between Fishguard and Waterford.

All of these last three ships are still afloat and in commission. The *St. Helier* returned to the Channel Islands service on Saturday, 15 June, 1946. First of the fleet to be released by the Government, she had been reconditioned for passenger use by South Wales firms. The *St. Julien*, which went to Penarth for her alterations, made her first post-war trip on Saturday, 30 November, 1946. She has space for 1,000 passengers, of whom 343 will have single or double cabins or open berths (there are also luxury cabins). The *St. Andrew*, refitted at Newport, carries 1,300; the number of state rooms has been increased from 16 to 24, and there are 350 berths altogether. Special attention has been given to the crew's quarters, which include additional mess rooms for the deck and engine-room ratings. All the furnishings and fittings for the two ships have been and are being supplied through South Wales firms ; South Wales also has been responsible during the last eighteen months for refitting the cargo ships *Great Western, Sambur,* and *Roebuck,* and the two tenders *Sir Richard Grenville* and *Sir John Hawkins.*

To replace the lost vessels, the Great Western has ordered two new ships each of three thousand tons. The new ships will have an overall length of 320 feet and a beam of 48 feet; and will accommodate 1,300 passengers, fifty motor-cars and 350 tons of freight. They will be constructed with a raked stem and cruiser stern and will have a speed of 21 knots. A rudder in the bow as well as the stern will facilitate manœuvring in a confined space.

Each of these ships will have sleeping quarters for four hundred in single, double or open berths in addition to luxury cabins fitted with private bathrooms and toilets. Special attention is being given to the standard of amenity in the third-class saloons and dining room, which will be large and airy and decorated in light and cheerful colours (see the illustration on page 96). Meals and snack-bar delicacies will be served in pleasant surroundings and the needs of families with children will be specially catered for. The ships, which will be planned so as to be easily adaptable to serve either the Irish or the Channel Islands traffic, are expected to be ready soon.

In this chapter on South Wales, the digression on ships may be justified by the fact that their control under the Chief Docks Manager is centred in that region. The chapter as a whole, however, with its account of railway lines and stations, of hotels and hostels, of ships and docks, clearly indicates that the Great Western's zeal in the service of South Wales remains as strong as ever. Without a doubt there are difficult times ahead, but on the subject of South Wales the Great Western is determined to side with the optimists. Its faith was well and simply expressed by the *Economist* in the spring of 1946. "South Wales," according to a leading article in that journal, "with many natural advantages and with a singularly adaptable labour force, has an unrivalled opportunity to regain its pre-1913 position as a leading industrial area." If by some unlucky chance the opportunity should be missed, no part of the fault is likely to attach to the Railway which, as Mr. David Grenfell, the Member for Gower, recently pointed out, "is doing a bigger job for Wales to-day than it has ever done before."

CHAPTER TEN · MINE HOST

___

THE HOTEL SERVICE

JUDGED by railway standards, the Great Western is not a large hotel owner, but its hotels have a reputation equal to that of the most famous and the most expensive. The Royal Hotel, Paddington, and the Tregenna Castle Hotel at St. Ives, in particular, are well known to those travellers who appreciate first-class service, comfortable beds and fine cookery and wines.

The service at these hotels has necessarily suffered some curtailment as a result of the war. The menus are of the standard wartime length; the well-known *a la carte* service at the Royal Hotel, Paddington (as also at a certain number of station restaurants) is still in abeyance because of food restrictions and shortage of staff. The Great Western intends at the earliest possible moment to reinstate all such amenities on a pre-war basis. In other directions, its plans provide for a substantial advance on the general pre-war standard, as, for example, the provision of more private bathrooms and improved arrangements for room service of meals. The practice of including a service charge on bills in lieu of gratuities has been adopted throughout the Great Western catering establishments, including hotels and restaurant cars, except for purchases "over the counter."

RENOVATIONS

It is probable that several years will elapse before labour and materials for the building of new hotels can be made available. The renovation of existing hotels must be the Company's first consideration. Concurrently with this work it is intended to carry out certain improvements and enlargements, the need for which has been manifest for some time past.

The biggest enterprise will be the rehabilitation of the Grand Pump Room Hotel at Bath, a recent acquisition. Increased accommodation will be provided by the demolition of the older part of the premises in Westgate Street, and the rebuilding there of a new wing to the full height of the main block. Each of the 178 bedrooms will have its own private bathroom; there will be also a few suites of rooms with well-furnished sitting-rooms. The ground floor will be replanned; the main lounge hall will be increased in size, and a new, spacious dining-room will be provided with direct access from the main hall. Over the dining-room there will be a new block of sixty bedrooms. Special lifts are to be installed for invalids. Visitors will also have access direct from the hotel to the Royal Baths. As far as furnishings are concerned, the Grand Pump Room Hotel will be, in effect, a brand new hotel; nothing is now left of the old furniture. An interesting modern feature is the smokeless all-gas installation for central heating, hot water and cooking.

In the recent war, a bedroom floor of the Royal Hotel, Paddington – fortunately the least comfortable – was gutted by German incendiaries. The reconstructed floor will have seventy modern bedrooms, each with hot and cold water, electric clocks, telephones, sockets for electric shavers, and other modern conveniences. There are also to be new and improved pantries and service lifts to meet the growing demand for the service of residents' meals in bedrooms.

At the favourite Tregenna Castle Hotel at St. Ives, Cornwall, a new block of garages is to be built with modern bedrooms for chauffeurs and hotel staff – all of them, of course, single bedrooms with hot and cold water. Other staff accommodation will include a dining-room and rest rooms. The herd of Jersey cattle have returned to the Home Farm where they were a familiar sight with visitors some years before the war. Later, the Farm will have brand-new cowsheds to house them; elsewhere new piggeries and other improvements will help to make the group of farm buildings one of the best equipped in the neighbourhood. As soon as the Ministry of Food can be induced to relax its austerity Orders, hotel guests will once again enjoy the sight of the brown earthenware pots of Cornish cream which adorned the dining room tables in happier days.

The stately Manor House Hotel, Moretonhampstead, was derequisitioned by the Government in the autumn of 1945 and was reopened to visitors on 1 October, 1946. For many years past the demand for accommodation at this hotel has been far above its resources, and the extensions planned include a new wing with forty bedrooms, mostly single and all, of course, with private bathrooms. The whole of another hotel – the Fishguard Bay Hotel, which lies on the edge of the beautiful Pembrokeshire cliffs – is being overhauled and redecorated. Though its main function is to cater for the needs of travellers for the Irish Channel passage, those in search of a restful holiday have been discovering this pleasant retreat in increasing numbers.

HOLIDAYS : NEW STYLE

At various times, many different interests aware of the high quality of its hotel services have pressed the Great Western to build additional hotels. There is at present an acute shortage of accommodation, more especially for the holiday and tourist traffics. The large increase in traffic resulting from an extension of holidays with pay, and the urgent need of attracting tourists from abroad, will necessarily involve the railways in many new activities. The Great Western, however, has decided that in the national interest it must concentrate on hotels for business people, the need for which is specially felt in the big towns of South Wales. Measured by its pre-war hotels organisation, the Company's hotel programme is an important one.

But mention must first be made of the one exception – the projected holiday hotel at Looe in Cornwall, a residential hotel in the true Great Western tradition. A beautiful site a couple of miles east of Looe was purchased some little time before the recent war. It lies four hundred feet above sea level. The views over the sea are magnificent and it has been the architect's first object to ensure that they are freely enjoyed from all the public rooms. The building will be carried out in traditional Cornish materials, and will probably be partly on two floors and partly on three, with between fifty and sixty bedrooms. The grounds are considerable, and the hotel will actually stand in an eighteen-hole golf course over the layout of which considerable trouble is being taken.

In the matter of holiday accommodation, the Great Western hopes during the next few years to do something not only to meet the greatly increased demand for high-class hotel accommodation, but also to cater for the more varied requirements of the modern holidaymaker. In conjunction with the other railway companies, it has informed the Government that it is prepared, within the limitations laid down by Parliament, to co-operate in schemes for the provision of low-cost hotel accommodation and of youth hostels and holiday camps. The limitation is mainly one of location. The Railway is free to provide accommodation of every possible type within a distance of five miles from any of the stations: beyond that distance it is not permitted to go.

At least one holiday camp is planned for the Great Western system. A number of sites in Wales (and also one or two elsewhere) are under consideration. The construction and management of the camp will be in the hands of Messrs. Thomas Cook & Son Ltd., who have been invited by the four railway companies to undertake responsibility for the holiday camps that will be sponsored by them. The camp in its layout and its general amenities will be generally similar to Messrs. Cook's existing camp at Prestatyn in North Wales.

The account of the Great Western's post-war plans for hotel developments would not be complete without some reference to the preliminary studies which are being made for a new type of family hotel. It has been repeatedly pointed out that under existing conditions those sections of the population who are able to take the fullest advantage of holiday provisions are those who are least in need of holidays. By common consent, holidays are, above all, necessary to the household where a young family is being raised; yet it is precisely this type of household that bulks overwhelmingly largest among the stay-at-homes. The Great Western has made detailed investigations into the needs of the family with growing children, and a tentative plan for an experimental family hotel is the outcome of these investigations. Charges would necessarily be low. An essential part of the scheme would be a twenty-four hour nursery service, staffed by experienced nurses, that could leave fathers and mothers free to seek rest and relaxation at any hour of the day or night. A hotel of this kind would meet a social need of outstanding importance, and its development would undoubtedly be watched with interest by social workers, by the trade unions, and by employers interested in the well-being of the homes to which their workers return each night.

BUSINESS HOTELS

The new Great Western business hotels at Cardiff and Swansea are part of the Railway's development plans for South Wales. Other new hotels are projected for Swindon and Birmingham.

The need for a first-class commercial hotel in Cardiff has been the subject of much comment. The new Great Western Hotel is planned on six floors giving a total of two hundred bedrooms (thirty double and 170 single), each with private bathroom. Manufacturers and others will be especially interested in the stock rooms which are to be provided for the private display of commercial goods.

The site at Swansea is one of the finest in the town. It lies between the civic centre and the sea and forms a corner on the circus to be constructed in front of the civic centre under the latest town-planning scheme. The preliminary design for the exterior of this hotel is reproduced on page 93. Most of the bedrooms will look out in a south-westerly direction across the sea to the Mumbles. There will be something under two hundred bedrooms, each with its private bathroom. Downstairs, guests will make their choice between the hotel dining-room and the restaurant, where they will find a dance floor and a band. For special occasions the two may be opened up into one large room seating three hundred altogether. A spacious public tea lounge is included in the ground floor plan, as well as a complete suite of bars – lounge, snack, saloon and public. On the first floor, the public rooms of the hotel will open direct on to a broad open terrace looking out over the sea. The garage will take ninety cars.

At Swindon, a smaller hotel will form part of the new group of station buildings. There will be about seventy bedrooms here; on the top floor will be a self-contained hostel for refreshment room staff, with single bedrooms, recreation rooms and the usual adjuncts. The hotel will be linked with the booking hall and platform by a covered way.

In the year before the war, a scheme was approved for providing an up-to-date hotel in connection with the reconstruction of the divisional office buildings at Snow Hill, Birmingham, at an estimated cost of £132,000. The scheme had to be deferred on account of the war. The Birmingham Corporation have recently prepared a town-planning scheme which involves the reconsideration of the whole of the proposals. At the same time, plans are being developed for additional improvements to the station. The hotel plan will be recast as soon as its general outline can be determined in relation to these larger schemes.

This group of hotels represents a new departure for the Great Western. Its older hotels are especially popular with families in search of relaxation. In them you may hear the laughter of children and breathe the smell of the sea or the moors. Will this gay and leisurely atmosphere survive in these new places where business men will be gathering to discuss the serious problems of life? That the tradition and experience of the Railway's experts will result in business hotels with a difference may certainly be taken for granted. Perhaps something like the charm and graciousness of the Royal Hotel, Paddington, may yet come to enliven the severity of the hard-working industrial towns of the Midlands and the West.

CONCLUSION

W<small>HAT</small>, at a final glance, is to be said about the picture that emerges from these pages? Sharp and clear in places, in others tentative and less distinct, it shows a multitude of interlocking human activities that at first seems baffling in its complexity. But the picture, if it is a true one, should indicate also how these activities are gathered together to a single end: the physical renewal of a public service that is old enough to be a national institution yet young enough to face its new responsibilities in a spirit of undiminished hope and ardour.

To improve the service to the traveller, to raise it to the level of the knowledge and the potentialities of our time, is the governing purpose. More and finer trains; brighter, cleaner compartments with stronger and better distributed lighting; stations worthy of their important position in the general civic scene; trains and stations from first to last an example of good taste, good craftsmanship, a fit environment for gracious living; such are the objects this Railway has set itself for the years immediately ahead. New coaches are to be built at the rate of some two or three hundred a year; at least twenty new stations are on the first programme. For the industrial community there are to be 2,400 new freight wagons by the end of 1947, thirty-one modernised goods stations, and new types of organisation including a network of thirty-four concentration points for the overnight delivery of small consignments of goods.

The programme would be an ambitious one at any time; in a period of shortage and frustration such as the present it might almost be described as audacious. It is a programme that calls for great feats of organisation and a high output of work in many branches of industry. Most exacting of all demands, perhaps, is the demand for the design and manufacture of hundreds of new and improved varieties of engines and tools, from the largest to the smallest; gas turbine locomotives embodying the results of the research and practical experience which the war made possible on an unprecedented scale; oil-burning locomotives to draw passenger and goods trains with greater regularity and efficiency than ever before; Diesel-electric locomotives to stand always ready for immediate work in the shunting yards; new devices which will bring the superb safety machinery of Automatic Train Control still nearer to perfection; new machines and power-operated tools for hauling goods in goods stations and yards; for digging, pumping, hoisting and other engineering operations; machines for prefabricating coaches and for lifting and laying prefabricated track; machines for performing scores of different operations in the building of new structures and the repairing and maintaining of the old.

And while these great projects get under way there still remains to be completed the long, grim job of rebuilding all branches of the railway service to the pre-war standard of volume, speed and quality; of reinstating all the old passenger and express goods services and of resuming the meticulous timekeeping of the past not only for a few trains but for all. The successful completion of this job means nothing less than the recovery, in the shortest possible time, of the millions of lost man-hours sacrificed in the all-out war effort. There are hundreds of war-damaged stations and other buildings to be repaired, thousands of wartime structures, installations, and pieces of equipment finally to be cleared away; railway track, locomotives, coaches, wagons, road vehicles, buildings, and installations of every kind to be treated with overhauls, repairs or renewals long postponed and overdue; surfaces everywhere, internal and external, to be cleaned, washed, restored and painted after six years of overwork, neglect and insidious deterioration.

How will these things be brought about? There will have to be a good deal of planning in offices and workshops, and much will depend on the energy and driving force of the managers and experts in charge. Scarce materials and specialised tools will have to be obtained under the most difficult circumstances. Often the approval of public authorities will be necessary before any move can be made. But the most important factor in the situation is the spirit that animates the 119,000 men and women of the Great Western on whose work the ultimate result must depend. Fortunately, this is a matter in which there is no uncertainty or possible doubt. These people know what has to be done, and they firmly intend to see their business brought to an early conclusion.

The truth is that railway work is something more than an occupation; it is an occupation having the power of an incentive. Much is being said and written in these days about incentives to work. The economists warn us that these incentives are the motive force that make the industrial machine go round, and that if they should dry up or weaken the machine would slow down and maybe come to a standstill. They tell us that there are two such incentives, which may be present either singly or in combination. "The human donkey," in the words of one authority, "requires either a carrot in front or a stick behind to goad it into activity." In other words, we must either be drawn by hope or driven by fear; without one of these there can be no forward motion. The potency of carrots and sticks is undeniable, but equally undeniable is the existence of a third incentive with which strict believers in the doctrine of economic man are perhaps less familiar. This incentive may shortly be described as vocation.

Vocation has little to do with hope, still less with fear; it has a great deal to do with another human attribute to which in unguarded moments we may sometimes refer as love. The man with a vocation is interested in the question whether his work is worth while rather than in the question whether it is likely to be worth *his* while. He is more concerned about the danger of losing his soul than he is about the danger of losing his job. It is a significant fact that though a poet once spoke of "dog-loyalty," no one discussing the attitude of the man with a vocation has yet felt it useful to compare him to a donkey. In the many difficult and dangerous achievements recorded in the pages of history, the incentive of vocation has not been altogether without effect; yet its power does not in any way depend on the presence of difficulty or danger. In every walk and every situation of life it is a force to be reckoned with, a force that can serve us certainly no less well than the heaviest of sticks or the most glittering of carrots. As far as this country is concerned, it may be that its prosperity in the years to come will depend less on our exploitation of material incentives than on our ability to seize and develop the potentialities of this mysterious moral force.

As an example of the power of vocation the railways of England are of absorbing interest. There cannot be many other forms of employment in which it counts for so much. In all the history of the Great Western folk its importance has never been challenged. These men of Middlesex and Berkshire, of the Westerly counties and Wales, are attached to their work and proud of it as were their fathers and grandfathers before them. They could not perform their tasks with such unfailing cheerfulness if they had not been drawn to them by something stronger than fear of loss. The work appeals to them in its interest and variety; it brings them into touch with people as few other occupations do. The more thoughtful might say with John Stuart Mill that "the main branch of the education of human beings is their habitual employment", and add that few forms of employment provide an education of quite the same high quality. Others might recall the days when the coming of the railways brought new life and prosperity to a country in imminent danger of economic collapse. Perhaps it was the memory of those days that in the last war called forth so quickly and so powerfully what Mr. Winston Churchill has described as "the grim determination, unwavering courage and constant resourcefulness of the railwaymen of all ranks"; perhaps it is the same memory that still causes the true Great Westerner to look upon his work as a form of public service that is part of the enduring tradition of his race.

EVOLUTION OF A DELIVERY ZONE

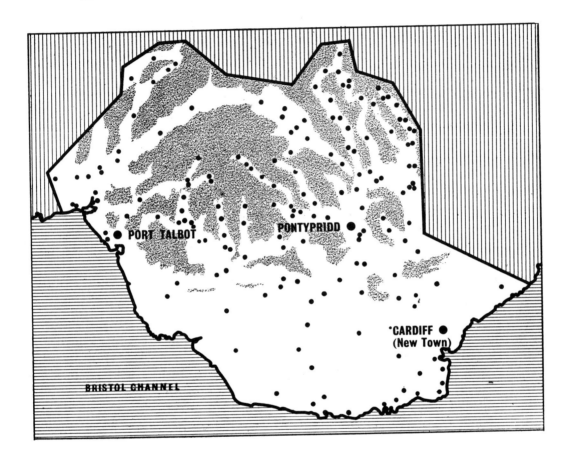

ONE

BEFORE 1927, consignments of goods in the Cardiff-Pontypridd-Port Talbot triangle in South Wales were carried to or from 156 Great Western stations by rail. The valley contours largely determined the shape of the railway network (see pp. 24-26).

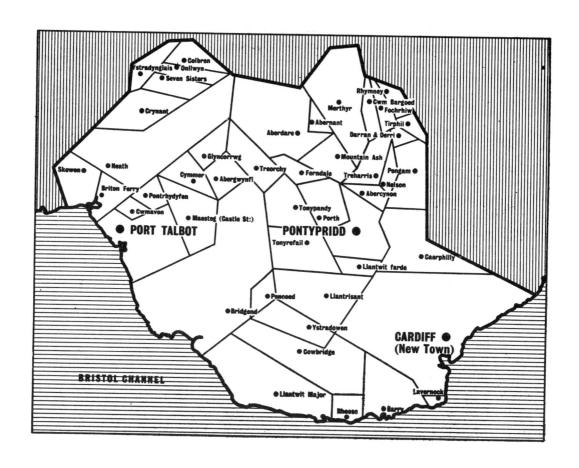

TWO

IN 1927, a plan was introduced under which the traffic previously
handled by 156 stations was to be gradually concentrated at
46 stations, from which goods would be collected and sent out
by road.

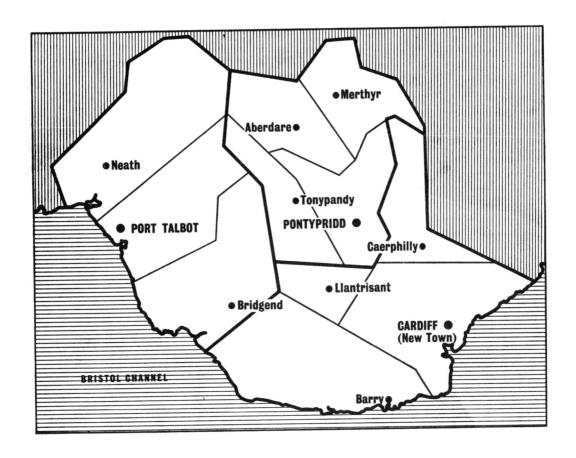

THREE

IN 1946, the concentration plan was replaced by the new zonal system. The 46 delivery areas were amalgamated into eleven delivery areas grouped in three zones, with railheads at Cardiff, Pontypridd and Port Talbot.